EUROPEAN
contemporary
CLASSICS
THEATRE

Of the first edition of this book, five hundred copies have been specially casebound and of these two hundred have been signed by the author, Eugenio Barba, and numbered.

LAND OF ASHES
AND DIAMONDS

EUGENIO BARBA

LAND OF ASHES
AND DIAMONDS

My Apprenticeship
in Poland

Followed by

26 Letters
from Jerzy Grotowski
to Eugenio Barba

Land of Ashes and Diamonds
Translated from the Italian
by Judy Barba

Grotowski's Letters
Translated from the Polish
by Eugenio and Judy Barba

First published in 1999
by Black Mountain Press
Centre for Performance Research
8 Science Park · Aberystwyth
SY23 3AH · Wales · UK

Typeset in Berkeley Old Style
Printed and Bound in Great Britain by
The Lavenham Press, Suffolk
Designed at The Design Stage · Cardiff Bay · Wales

British Library Cataloguing in Publication Data
A catalogue record for this book is available from the British
Library

Library of Congress Cataloguing in Publication Data
A catalogue record for this book has been requested

ISBN 1 902867 00 9 (hbk)
ISBN 1 902867 01 7 (pbk)

European Contemporary Classics
Series Editor : Richard Gough

BLACK MOUNTAIN PRESS
Black Mountain Press is a division of
the Centre for Performance Research Ltd

To Poland
where I learned that theatre is struggle
and a longing for freedom

On the tip of the branch

high on the highest bough

the apple blushes red

forgotten at harvest time

by the farmers.

But it was not forgotten.

In vain they tried to reach it.

Sappho

CONTENTS

I

LAND OF ASHES AND DIAMONDS
My Apprenticeship in Poland

Preamble 9
Aknowledgements 13
Postscript 13

A Film which Changes Lives 15
Friends 16
Travels 18
Opole 23
Archetypes and Shamans 26
Crossing Deserts and Hitchhiking 33
The Theatre's New Testament 38
Relationships and Chess Games 42
A Thousand and One Nights 46
Pulsation, Rhythm, Movement 52
Censors and Allies 58
How to Be Both Dove and Snake 61
The Value of a Bus 68
First Flashback 75
In Search of Theatre 75
The Friendless Hamlet 76
Persona Non Grata 84
Second Flashback 86
Hungering for Theatre 89
Holstebro 92
Towards a Poor Theatre 97
The Last Production 102
The Invisible Master 104
A Question Unanswered 108
A Few is the Right Number 113

II

DEAR KIM
26 Letters from Jerzy Grotowski to Eugenio Barba

Letter 1 *(10 July 1963)* 117
Letter 2 *(15 September 1963)* 119
Letter 3 *(21 September 1963)* 122
Letter 4 *(undated, probably end of November 1963)* 124
Letter 5 *(undated, probably end of December 1963 or beginning of January 1964)* 125
Letter 6 *(12 May 1964)* 126
Letter 7 *(4 July 1964)* 129
Letter 8 *(1 September 1964)* 130
Letter 9 *(2 September 1964)* 133
Letter 10 *(3 September 1964)* 134
Letter 11 *(20 October 1964)* 135
Letter 12 *(29 December 1964)* 138
Letter 13 *(6 February 1965)* 140
Letter 14 *(5 April 1965)* 143
Letter 15 *(26 April 1965)* 145
Letter 16 *(8 June 1965)* 148
Letter 17 *(20 June 1965)* 150
Letter 18 *(5 September 1965)* 152
Letter 19 *(27 September 1965)* 155
Letter 20 *(16 November 1965)* 157
Letter 21 *(18 December 1965)* 160
Letter 22 *(14 January 1966)* 161
Letter 23 *(5 December 1966)* 164
Letter 24 *(23 April 1967)* 166
Letter 25 *(21 September 1967)* 168
Letter 26 *(10 August 1969)* 169

Illustrations 173

Name Index 177

IN APRIL 1994, on an out-of-the-way shelf in my library, I found twenty-six letters that Jerzy Grotowski had written to me between July 1963 and August 1969. They are probably not all of his letters from that period, but it is no coincidence that the first one was sent to me while I was in India, and the last from India, during his first trip there.

India was for us a point of encounter. We never set foot there together, but from our very first meeting its culture, its paradoxes, its close remoteness established between us a bond of thought and a common language.

Most of the letters date from 1964 to 1966. For Grotowski these were the years preceding the explosion of his fame, and for me those of the foundation and establishment of Odin Teatret in Oslo, Norway, and then in Holstebro, Denmark.

After 1970 our correspondence became less frequent. Grotowski's prestige abroad made it easier for him to leave Poland. After the Teatr-Laboratorium 13 Rzędów's move from Opole to Wrocław, the country's regime had softened. It became less complicated to meet outside Poland, either in Holstebro or elsewhere in Europe. Our work commitments often made it simpler to telephone rather than write. In other words, the dwindling in our correspondence was a sign of easier rather than less frequent contact. This happened at the same time that our paths diverged.

All my energy was concentrated on training the actors in my group, on creating a performance, on finding the venues and contacts to present it, on inventing and carrying out activities which could justify the designation 'laboratory' which I had given to Odin Teatret. It was a matter of ensuring the material and professional survival of a group of very young actors, who were amateurs and autodidacts of differing nationalities and languages. These preoccupations were far removed from those of Grotowski. At that particular moment, he was haunted by very different tensions. At the end of 1970 he made public his decision not to make any more productions.

My letters to Grotowski were kept in the files of the Teatr-Laboratorium in Wrocław. When Ludwik Flaszen and the actors declared its closure in 1984, while Grotowski was living abroad as a stateless person, they were lost. I can only publish here a depleted correspondence.

Grotowski and I have spoken at length about these letters, about the world which they conjure up, the net of dissimulations and the secret code which, on the one hand are an attempt to escape the eye of the police, while on the other give a naive and novel-like patina to our enthusiasm, our discoveries and our reciprocal solidarity, half way between Lancelot (or Percival) and Rocambole. Sometimes it has been difficult even for us to decipher our past code. Now we can smile about it, yet we cannot forget that it was a true adventure, and a gamble whose stakes were the closure of the Teatr 13 Rzędów.

I have asked myself whether this adventure is comprehensible to today's reader. I erected barriers of doubt against the project to publish the letters. Could they have a meaning over and above the interest that any document involving a personality such as Grotowski would inevitably arouse?

I have never placed much value on relics. Museums fascinate me, but I cannot bear to see people I have loved and still love enclosed in them; or even worse, to see pieces of my own life exhibited there.

But I have always loved history, its contradictions, the drama which ensues every time its ordered bookish surface comes into conflict with that which it involuntarily conceals.

In this way the barriers of doubt toppled over on me and were transformed into a new task. The twenty-six letters had to be preceded by a description which placed them in a context: Poland during that period, just as I had experienced it. I had to tell how, for me, a tiny provincial theatre had turned into a spiritual continent, a homeland of my own invention to which I could emigrate. A dream to which I could be loyal.

I had to attempt to explain how two young men, of almost the same age and not yet thirty years old, could conceive of their relationship in terms taken from Kipling, expressing it as the bond between the old Lama and the young Kim.

* * *

The first part of the book - *Land of Ashes and Diamonds* - tells a fragment of the subterranean history of the theatre and a love story.

I wrote it with the intention of providing a testimony to certain crucial years in the theatre of the second half of the twentieth century, with the incubation and the establishment of the theatre revolt by Jerzy Grotowski, Ludwik Flaszen, Jerzy Gurawski and the small group of actors around them. The context is socialist Poland, during a period in its history which was marked by the dreariness of a police regime and by the fervour of an intellectual and artistic life that was at the same time a liberating cry and a tireless fashioning of liberty.

Every trace of the fragrance of those years, not long past, seems today to have vanished. And as always when tracks fade, history runs the risk of becoming rectilinear, or in other words faintly distorted in spite of the truth of the facts which it connects together.

It is possible, for instance, to link Grotowski's theatre to the reforms and research of the first half of the century, along the Slavonic line: Stanislavsky-Vachtangov-Meyerhold-Eisenstein-Grotowski. Or else, more unusually, a line which follows the work of the actor and director *within* and *against* the literary text: Meyerhold-Brecht-Grotowski. Or again, a line going beyond the horizon of the performance seen as the unique objective of theatre work: Stanislavsky-Sulerzhitski-Copeau-Osterwa-Grotowski. All these connections are correct. But they are of use above all, to those who have given themselves the task of finding a meaning and a direction for the events of the past.

All these explanations are of no use to those who today find themselves in the situation of having to fight against adverse circumstances, indifference and solitude, with the need to invent a home - a theatre - for themselves on their own terms. They are not merely interested in the great current of twentieth century theatre history, the account of the victorious struggles which, from afar, appear to be aesthetic revolutions and fundamental discoveries. In the adventures of their predecessors, they also look for examples and inspiration to surmount the countless day-to-day obstacles and solve the arduous problems caused by their own choices. They search for stratagems, techniques, principles and ideals which may help them to overcome their own overwhelming inadequacy. For those who do not yet have a name, who are attempting to discover or win one, it is above all helpful to become acquainted with the prosaic material conditions, which characterised the story of other nameless ones.

Portbou is a Spanish village on the frontier with France where Walter Benjamin committed suicide while fleeing from Nazism. I went there in the spring of 1995 to visit his grave. I looked for it in the cemetery, but it was not to be found. Then, in a flash, I realised that it couldn't be there: not only had he committed suicide, but he was also a Jew.

The cemetery is situated high up on the rocky coast jutting out into the sea and sky. Not far away, protruding from the stony ground, was the entrance to a tunnel, like a steel intestine, built of the same heavy metal plating as a battleship and flaking with rust from the salty breezes. A staircase, also of steel, led down inside the tunnel as far as the sea. As I began walking down it, my own image came to meet me. In the distance I could see the blue-green of the water and at the same time I saw myself approaching. The tunnel ended abruptly, looking out over the sea, and closed by a pane of glass reflecting whoever descended the steps. I let my emotions flow as I admired the monument which Dani Karavan had dedicated to the Marxist cabalist, until my own reflection, in the barely opaque glass, halted my descent. Inscribed on the glass in tiny letters was a quotation from Walter Benjamin: *It is more arduous to honour the memory of the nameless than that of the renowned. Historical construction is devoted to the memory of the nameless.*

I would like to recount a central moment in theatre history as though it were the story of nameless young people. I want to present it for what it was at the time, a subterranean history, a story of moles. Were we fanatics dazzled by a mirage? Was it public recognition and celebrity that transformed this mirage into a diamond? The subterranean history of the theatre cannot be ensnared by clarity and reasonable *a posteriori* explanations. It is a flow of apparent fortuitousness, disconnected events and chance meetings. Above all it uncovers - behind the greatness of the results and the effectiveness of the choices - other forces and other dimensions: the impulse to revolt, the inability to bend with the spirit of the time, the thirst to transcend one's own society and self. And the force of falling in love and of love itself.

What name other than 'love' can we give to the passion which has bound certain theatre artists one to another, transforming into viable possibilities those ideas which dispassionate people considered at the time to be the obsessions of solitary maniacs? Was it not a love story between Sulerzhitski and Stanislavsky? And Vachtangov? Was it not a true story of unhappy and tempestuous love that nourished the relationship between Stanislavsky and Meyerhold? Or between Eisenstein and Meyerhold?

Today, passionate love is always seen in one dimension only: the erotic. For this reason it is virtually impossible to understand the term 'Master' in all its depth. It is difficult to penetrate beyond the obvious, beyond concepts such as influence, methods, lineage, fidelity or infidelity. As though the Master were not one who reveals himself, only to disappear. As though his action consisted only in teaching and seducing, instead of being the arduous introduction to the discovery of one's own creative solitude, without mourning.

Acknowledgements

It was Nando Taviani, dear friend and close collaborator for more than 25 years, who persuaded me to publish Grotowski's letters, preceding them with the story of those decisive years which I spent with my master in Opole. My Italian publisher Carla Carloni of Il Mulino has been a firm supporter of the book which seemed premature to me. I have discussed the language and tone with various friends who have had the patience to read the manuscript and the generosity to criticise it outspokenly: Julia Varley, Franco Ruffini, Nicola Savarese, Clelia Falletti, Rina Skeel, Ugo Volli, Stefano Geraci, Paolo Taviani, Roberto Tinti, Iben Nagel Rasmussen, Torgeir Wethal and Zbigniew Osiński. With the encouragement and competent help of Mirella Schino, and after a thousand hesitations, the book has finally reached its conclusion.

Carpignano, July 1996 - Holstebro, January 1998.

Postscript

When I wrote *Land of Ashes and Diamonds* Jerzy Grotowski was already seriously ill, but remained active and we were in regular contact. My last meeting with him was in November 1997 in Italy where he received an honorary doctorate from the University of Bologna. Once again we spoke of this book, which he had read in its Italian manuscript form. We discussed certain details and also the translation of his letters. *Land of Ashes and Diamonds* was first published in June 1998 in Italy. Jerzy Grotowski died in Pontedera, Italy, on 14th January 1999. His last wish was for his ashes to be taken to Arunachala in India, where Ramana Maharishi had his *ashram.*

I have decided not to make any changes in future editions but to allow Grotowski to appear in the book as if he were still alive.

Eugenio Barba
Holstebro, 25 January 1999

I

LAND OF ASHES AND DIAMONDS

My Apprenticeship in Poland

A Film which Changes Lives

It was Andrzej Wajda who convinced me to go to Poland. Or rather, Wajda made a film for the very purpose of making me study theatre in Poland. It was *Ashes and Diamonds* and I saw it in Oslo in the autumn of 1959. It hit me like a punch in the stomach and I went back to see it again and again: three, five, maybe ten times. The images that flashed onto the screen were of a civil war, of a desperate passion, of a sense of honour and a contempt for life, of a tenderness for the madness and the weakness of human beings crushed by the ferocity of history. The protagonist, Zbigniew Cybulski, had a virile yet vulnerable expression which I was to find again years later in the face of Grotowski's actor Ryszard Cieślak. The story took place in Poland, a country which until then had been for me as distant and abstract as Namibia or Moldavia. I knew only that it was a monarchy and that its king was called Ubu. Now Poland was embodied in those men and women who loved and who died as though they were a part of me.

Rushing to the library to read up something about this new discovery, I chanced upon an issue of Sartre's magazine *Les Temps Modernes* which was devoted to the 'Polish October', the bloodless insurrection of 1956 that had brought the liberal Gomułka to power. Texts by unknown poets, writers, philosophers and playwrights revealed to me a country of a thousand and one nights. I had to go there.

Armed with a scholarship to study Polish literature, I arrived in Warsaw in January 1961, straight from Israel where I had spent six months wandering around. I stepped off the train, my head filled with dreams and the firm intention to become a theatre director. I was twenty-four years old and didn't speak a word of Polish.

I enrolled at the University and then went to the theatre school to inquire about the entrance exam: a detailed project for a production including scenography and costumes, which they agreed to let me do in French. I chose Sophocles' *Oedipus Rex*.

I set to work on my production project while at the same time studying Polish. I also followed the courses at the University, and although I understood very little this gave me the opportunity to meet other young people, and in the evening go with them to student clubs. One of my professors was Jan Kott, a brilliant critic, still unknown abroad.

At the beginning of March I did the theatre school exam with Bohdan Korzeniewski, head of the faculty of theatre direction. My political commitment had transformed Sophocles' text into an 'optimistic tragedy'. I imagined a pyramid filling the whole stage with Oedipus, Jocasta, their children and Creon on the summit. The populace, and Tiresias the seer, were relegated to the lower steps. In the final scene, while Oedipus, his face covered in blood, was leaving Thebes, and Creon lamented his terrible destiny, the populace climbed the pyramid and drove Creon out: the time for individualism, when heroes solved enigmas and plunged the community into disaster was past.

My interpretation must have seemed very naive in Poland, and typical of a left-wing militant from a 'free' country in the West. Barely five years had passed since the Poles, after a long period of harsh Stalinist regime and through a risky confrontation with the Russians, had succeeded in bringing the liberal Władisław Gomułka back to power and partially liberating themselves from the dogmatism imposed by the Soviet Union. Korzeniewski listened patiently to my explanations, asking questions about the characters, their motivations, the costumes and the masks which were inspired by some Babylonian bas-reliefs. finally he asked me if I was sure that the performance should end as it did. Surprised, I replied that it was the very key to the topicality of *Oedipus Rex*. He then inquired how the whole population could have stood on that tiny summit. I was embarrassed, not understanding whether his objection was literal and referred to the number of the actors in the choir, or whether it contained an ironical subtext.

It was one of my first lessons in Poland on the painful opposition between wishful thinking and concrete thinking, between what we want and what reality forces upon us, between our day-dreams and the ruthless objectivity of history. 'All right, Barba, all right' – Korzeniewski said encouragingly – 'I think you can study in our school.'

Friends

I lived on Madalinskiego Street in a student hostel. On the first floor there were foreign students in single or double rooms, while the other floors were occupied only by girls, four to a room. My room-mate was a young

Argentinian composer, Romuald Peliński, who introduced me to contemporary Polish music – Szymanowski, Lutosławski, Penderecki – and dragged me along to the concerts of the Warsaw Autumn, a festival of modern music.

My inseparable companion was Erik Veaux, a Frenchman with a Swedish mother. He spoke Swedish very well and we amused ourselves by using it as a secret language. He was a Slavonic specialist, translator of Witkacy and Tadeusz Borowski, and his verve had opened the doors of the capital's artistic and literary circles. Through him I came to know Jerzy Andrzejewski and Jerzy Broszkiewicz, both well known writers, the young playwright Sławomir Mrożek and the elderly Artur Maria Swinarski, as well as the critics Artur Sandauer and Henryk Bereza, and Krzysztof Teodor Toeplitz, a well known expert on cinema. Sometimes I went to visit them alone, sometimes with Erik; more often we met at the Klub Literatów.

Often, in the evenings, Erik and I went to the Teatr Żydowski (Jewish Theatre), where the unforgettable Ida Kamińska performed in Yiddish, or else we visited the poet Miron Białoszewski who gave performances in his own home. The censors closed their eyes (which was typical of the situation at that time) while fifteen to twenty people, almost all artists or intellectuals, crowded into those two tiny rooms to watch Białoszewski enact his avant-garde texts, alone or with his slender friend, the painter Ludmiła Murawska.

They were months of lively activity, classes, discoveries, encounters, journeys and fun. I passed intense days between the theatre school and the university, with friends and people from the artistic milieu, and every evening going to one or two performances. Then supper or letting myself go at the SPATIF, the club for theatre people.

The effervescence of the artistic life was at its height in poetry, literature, the plastic arts, film, modern music, jazz, and theatre. Although I understood little Polish, the striking scenography and the quality of actors such as Halina Mikołajska, Irene Eichlerówna, Jacek Woszczerowicz, Gustaw Holoubek, Jan Świderski or Tadeusz Łomnicki were sufficient to hold my attention. Playwrights such as Jerzy Broszkiewicz, Tadeusz Różewicz and Sławomir Mrożek, directors like Erwin Axer, Bohdan Korzeniewski, Kazymierz Dejmek, Krystyna Skuszanka, or the young Konrad Swinarski and Jerzy Jarocki, the scenographers Jan Kosiński, Jósef Szajna, Tadeusz Kantor, Zenobiusz Strzelecki, Andrzej Stopka and Eva Starowieyska or the young Krystyna Zachwatowicz – every one of these artists guaranteed an evening in which I surprised myself by learning something new.

The variety and the quality of Polish theatre was unique in Europe and I felt it was my duty to help it be known and appreciated. I wrote long letters to my friends in other European countries and also made contact with *Sipario*, a theatre magazine in Milan, proposing to the editor, Benedetta Galassi Beria, an issue on Polish theatre. I included a list of the subjects to be dealt with, the names of possible collaborators and also two plays to be translated. She accepted. Thus my circle of acquaintances widened. I went to visit the magazines *Teatr*, *Dialog* and *Pamiętnik Teatralny* to ask for advice and articles from their directors, and I started doing interviews myself [1].

In 1961 there were not many foreigners in Poland and communication with people was easy. Even on entering a bar or a restaurant your 'western' clothes gave you away. Immediately there would be somebody ready to offer you a drink and enter into long discussions. Never before had I met such generous and hospitable people. I had a profound admiration for the Poles' resistance against the Germans during the war, for their hard life under the socialist regime, for their cultural policy which supported over a hundred and twenty theatres whose tickets cost the same as those for the cinema. I was intrigued by the vitality of these people, their *dostojewczysna* whose contagious energy transformed even me into a feverish Dostoevsky character.

Travels

I grasped every opportunity to become acquainted with theatres and directors from other towns. I visited Kazimierz Dejmek in Lódż and attended his rehearsals for a few days; I went to Gdańsk to a meeting of the Polish Students' Union where I came across the best student theatres, one of which was Co To in which Zbigniew Cybulski, the actor who had made such an impression on me in the film *Ashes and Diamonds*, had started his career.

In June I made a short trip to Cracow to see my Norwegian friend, Dag Halvorsen, who was studying sociology at the Jagielloński University.

---

[1] '*Sipario*' appeared as a double issue (208-209) in August 1963 with Franco Quadri as its editor. It contained articles by the critics Jan Kott, Jan Błoński, Konstanty Puzyna, Adam Tarn, Edward Csató, Maria Czanerle, Jan Kłossowicz, Tadeusz Kudliński, Wojciech Natanson, Andrzej Wirth, Andrzej Wróblewski, by the directors Erwin Axer, Krystyna Skuszanka and Lidia Zamkow-Słomczynska, by the scenographers Jósef Szajna, Zenobiusz Strzelecki, Jan Kosiński and Krystyna Zachwatowicz, texts by Witkacy and two plays, one by Tadeusz Różewicz and the other by Jerzy Broszkiewicz. Roland Grünberg, a French friend and graphic artist, wrote about Grotowski. I made a series of interviews with directors and scenographers and, under the pseudonym Gösta Marcus, wrote an article on the mime theatre of Henryk Tomaszewski.

Together we went to the performances of the Stary and Slowacki theatres, the student theatre '38' and then we finished off the evening at the *Piwnica Pod Baranami*, a controversial satirical cabaret where poets, singers and actors appeared.

The theatre I liked best was in Nowa Huta, a satellite town a few kilometres from Cracow created as the result of a gigantic five-year plan. Vast steelworks spewed out smoke amidst a dingy scenario of ugly blocks of flats, the worst examples of socialist architecture. The huge theatre, for the thousands of workers and their families, was directed by Kristina Skuszanka and her husband Jerzy Krasowski. Their productions were renowned for the quality of the texts and for their theatricality, thanks also to the scenographer Jósef Szajna. During the war, Szajna had been sent to Auschwitz. It was the first time I saw a number tattooed on a man's arm. On our very first meeting he invited me to his home and showed me his studio. We often met and drank late into the night. With him I was often a prey to contrasting reactions. It was as if I stood before a ghost who reminded me of the horrors of history, and at the same time I was facing Orpheus who had escaped death and hell with his soul intact. I was impressed with his artistic vitality, the ardour with which he discussed, his capacity to drink countless glasses of vodka (and I had seen how Poles could drink), his hunger for life and his impetuous attraction to women.

At the end of my stay in Cracow I decided to return to Warsaw via Wrocław, a town that in spite of still being scarred by the ruins of the war, was nevertheless universally praised for its beauty. I wanted to visit the Teatr Polski and meet its director, Jakub Rotbaum. Dag Halvorsen, my Norwegian friend, decided to accompany me. His girlfriend, Janka Katz, a young Jewish critic and poet [2], said when she heard our plans: 'Why don't you stop in Opole? A friend of mine, Jerzy Grotowski, lives there and directs the avant-garde Teatr 13 Rzędów together with Ludwik Flaszen'. I had never heard the name of Grotowski, but that of Flaszen was familiar to me. In spite of his proverbial reluctance to put pen to paper, he was nevertheless considered to be one of the best literary and theatre critics together with Konstanty Puzyna, Andrzej Kijowski and Jan Błoński. His first book, *The Head and the Wall*, had been confiscated by the censors. However, a few rare copies circulated underground, revealing Flaszen's critical attitude towards official literature and its criteria.

Dag and I thought it not a bad idea to stop in Opole to meet Flaszen, as when we foreigners visited provincial theatres the directors were always

---

[2] Janka emigrated to Denmark in 1969 when a new 'anti-zionist' policy made life impossible for the few Jews who had survived Nazi extermination.

hospitable and offered us food and drink. We arrived in Opole in the afternoon and, on Rynek, the main square, discovered with some difficulty the
Teatr 13 Rzędów. Through a small door, we entered a short narrow
corridor which also served as a foyer and led into a room which was no
more than eighty square metres in size. They were performing *Dziady*
(The Forefathers) by Adam Mickiewicz, one of the greatest romantic poets
of the nineteenth century who, in the eyes of his compatriots, incarnated
the revolt and the defence of their national culture in a Poland which was
split between Russia, Prussia and Austria.

It must have been the premiere because Tadeusz Kudliński, the critic
for the Cracow newspaper *Dziennik Polski* was there. Dag and I met
Grotowski and Flaszen before the performance and greeted them from
Janka Katz. Grotowski was a tall young man, somewhat corpulent, with a
formal manner and dressed in black from top to toe (black trousers,
jacket, shirt, tie, shoes, socks and a pair of sunglasses which he wore even
during the performance and at night). He looked like a Protestant priest.
Flaszen was shorter in stature, plump, warm and ironical, with a small
beard à la Lenin. He made me think of Mephistopheles embodied in a
schoolteacher so as not to attract attention in a small provincial socialist
town.

The performance took place in that room of eighty square metres.
There was no stage. The spectators, about forty in all, were scattered
around and the actors moved about amongst them. Three girls were
seated in the centre, and at a certain point they were dragged out of the
room by the actors amid the embarrassment and laughter of everyone.
The actors were made up in an exaggerated way, some of them with long
false beards. They were very young, all of them under thirty.

Accustomed as I was to the sophisticated scenography and theatrical
quality of many Polish productions, this *Dziady* struck me as unpolished.
I was annoyed by the proximity of the actors forcing me to notice the
seams in a costume, the patch of perspiration on a shirt, a false beard
beginning to peel off a chin. The actors' direct contact with the audience,
and the inclusion of some spectators in the action, were reminiscent of
student cabarets where this was an accepted convention. In *Dziady* I did
not encounter that which for me was an essential part of the theatrical
experience: the dual effect of emotional participation and intellectual
distance.

In short, the first performance by Grotowski that I had seen, had left
me indifferent. The fact that the separation between stage and audience
had been abolished and that the actors moved around among the

spectators did not make any great impression on me. After all, it was as if the closeness to the audience, typical of Białoszewski's performances in his home or those at the *Piwnica Pod Baranami* in Cracow, reappeared also in this small theatre in Opole. The style of acting also bothered me, recalling the work of amateurs who were overacting or parodying a text.

I had the impression that the actors and the director took themselves tremendously seriously. There were scenes which seemed to me to border on a lack of taste, or in which I saw good ideas that remained at an intellectual level. In one of them the protagonist, Zygmunt Molik, walked bent under a broom as though it were a cross. Without doubt, such an image aroused ambiguous and conflicting resonances in the Polish spectators: on the one hand the profanation of a well known drama, and on the other the allusions to Tsarist Russia which were still valid under the Soviet oppression. Until recently, that fragment of the text had been censored. Analysing that very scene, the critic Tadeusz Kudliński wrote that Grotowski had imposed a dialectic of apotheosis and derision on Mickiewicz's text. This formulation was immediately adopted by Grotowski who considered it to be the best description of his way of approaching classical texts.

After the performance, Dag and I spoke briefly with Grotowski, but he was evidently busy with Kudliński and other guests. We went back to our hotel, and the next day we continued to Wrocław. There we wandered around amongst the ruins of that beautiful city and visited the Teatr Polski, where we were also treated to a good lunch by the director, Jakub Rotbaum.

The summer came around, and the university and theatre school closed for the holidays. I had to decide how to pass the summer months. Leszek Woźniak, who was engaged to an Iranian girl studying medicine and living in the same student hostel as me, came with the solution. He was an engineer and worked in the sugar refinery at Chełmża, near Toruń, the birthplace of Copernicus. He suggested I might help in the workers' social club, perhaps organising some theatre. Being keen to get to know other circles apart from students and artists, I proposed instead that he find me a job in his factory. So I spent a month as a welder, the trade I had learnt in Norway. Then I joined up with a brigade of 'voluntary' workers who, as was the normal practice under socialist regimes, were going off to the country to help the peasants with the harvest. I returned to Warsaw with all my muscles aching.

I had been moved to another student hostel in the Square of the Heroes of the Ghetto. It was right in the centre of what had been Warsaw's Jewish

21

quarter which the Germans had totally demolished after the Jewish uprising in 1943. I went back to studying at the theatre school and the university whenever I could, perfecting my Polish, and spending the evenings at the theatre and the nights with friends.

The grey autumn sky shrouded the city and my mind in shadow. Warsaw still bore the traces of the war. Its reconstruction progressed slowly, but the restaurants and night spots exploded with the joy of living. After performances, the actors went to the SPATIF Club which remained open until two o'clock in the morning. They were jovial, thanks to the vodka, the food and that special exaltation that follows fatigue. Often they would move on to the Hotel Bristol whose bar closed at dawn. In the streets, hundreds of tiny lights burned amongst the ruins. On the walls, lit up by those small flames, one could read the names of the Poles who had been killed during the German occupation.

Warsaw was gloomy, with long queues outside the shops selling vital food and supplies. Bulldozers dug amongst the ruins, turning up bones which were taken away by the lorry-load. My enthusiasm for Poland melted like snow in the sun. In this society which defined itself as socialist, my left-wing ideas collided with endless examples of injustice, abuse of power, bureaucracy, indifference and cynicism. My ingenuousness vanished, and in its place I felt acquiescence and apathy creeping in. I was confused. All my theories, both political and theatrical, dissolved. I felt alone and unprotected, unable to dispel a feeling of dejection in spite of throwing myself headfirst into the pursuit of studies, amusement and continuous love affairs.

I spoke of my state of mind to my friends. They comforted me, themselves admitting to being depressed by conditions in Poland. It seemed to me, however, that they were able to breathe whereas I was suffocating. I had come to Poland because I believed that 'communism restored its fertility to the human race'. But, as I saw it, socialism was an obscene caricature, often even a nightmare.

It was Barry Clayton who instilled in me the will to keep going. He was an English communist, about ten years older than me, and worked for Radio Poland, doing their English language broadcasts. He begged me not to let myself go, to be beaten by the depression and give up. I had to stay in Poland. He had also gone through a similar crisis after about a year, as indeed did every foreigner, every sensitive communist. I simply had to prolong my scholarship, continue my studies, finish the four years of theatre school, carry on for as long as possible. Was it not an objective fact that Polish theatre was the best in Europe?

Urged on by him, I requested an extension of my scholarship from the Italian government. At the end of the year I received the news that it had been granted.

Opole

One October day I decided to visit my Norwegian friend Dag Halvorsen in Cracow. Without any particular motive I got off the train halfway, in Opole, and went back to the Teatr 13 Rzędów. There was no performance that evening. Later on I realised that its season was intermittent because of a lack of spectators. Since 1959 when the direction of the theatre had been entrusted to Grotowski and Flaszen, its repertoire had consisted of avant-garde authors like Cocteau or Mayakovsky, or else classics such as Byron or the Indian Kalidasa. They were not the most popular authors in Opole, a working-class town in Silesia, whose conspicuous German minority had been expelled after the war and replaced by Polish refugees from the eastern territories which Russia had annexed.

When I arrived, Grotowski was at the theatre and he appeared more affable than at our first meeting. We went off to a restaurant called *Pająk*, The Spider, to talk. Here we began to weave the web of our relationship, spinning it over an abyss of dark and luminous forces - longings, needs and certainties. An inner space to which we can give different names: a journey into the depths of our own being, or an escape from it.

Grotowski was then twenty-eight, three years older than me, but his theatrical experience was already considerable. During the two previous years he had directed twelve productions in Opole, Cracow, Poznań, and even a radio performance in Cracow. Some of the Opole productions were montages built around local topics, obviously presented in order to hold the authorities at bay and satisfy norms of production.

He knew how to expound his arguments - theatre, politics, religion and philosophy - forcefully and with conviction. He had a sense of humour and a remarkable propensity for witticisms and wordplay. In 1955 after completing the four years of theatre school in Cracow as an actor, he was straightaway awarded a scholarship to follow a one-year course in direction at GITIS, the Institute for Performing Arts, in Moscow. His teacher was Yuri Zavadsky who had been an actor with Vachtangov and Stanislavsky.

Many years later, in 1994 in Holstebro, Grotowski spoke to me for a whole night about Yuri Zavadsky, the grandson of a Polish aristocrat who had been deported to Siberia during the Warsaw insurrection of 1863. He had played Kalaf in the legendary *Princess Turandot* of 1922. He was a well known and highly acclaimed artist. His work with the actors was excellent, but his productions were in the worst socialist-realistic style and had won him innumerable honours. He was a severe and irritable teacher, especially towards the Poles, but he had taken a liking to Grotowski.

There were two Mongolian students at GITIS. One day, infuriated by one of them who had some difficulty in understanding Russian, Zavadsky had broken off his lesson. He was already in his car when a delegation of students led by Grotowski approached to beg him to come back. At the first opportunity Grotowski went up to him and whispered: 'You should be angry with the other Mongol who is an informer.'

At the party to celebrate the end of the first year of the course (which lasted five years) Zavadsky remained silent. Then he made a single toast: 'To Jerzy Grotowski who has understood how long one should study at GITIS'. In fact, after his year of scholarship, Grotowski was to return to Poland.

Zavadsky believed that there were generations which created and generations which were witnesses. During the official ceremony of rehabilitation for Tairov, Grotowski had asked him when it would be Meyerhold's turn. Zavadsky had replied harshly: 'Meyerhold was a formalist and a cosmopolitan whose defeats, though merited, were more significant than all our greatest victories.'

Only once had Zavadsky invited Grotowski to his home: innumerable spacious rooms, filled with antique furniture. There was nothing in these luxurious surroundings that might recall the socialist regime except for a small statuette of Felix Dzerzhinsky, a Pole who was one of the protagonists of the October Revolution. He was also the founder and first head of the CEKA, the secret police and predecessor of the NKVD and of the present-day KGB. Glancing at the statuette, Zavadsky had remarked with a wink: 'If nothing else, at least he was a Pole.'

Then he had opened a drawer and shown Grotowski his passport, a document that nobody possessed in a socialist country: 'I can go to Capri or to London tomorrow if I want to see a show in the West End.' He had led him to the window and pointed out two large ZIM limousines parked in the courtyard, each with its own chauffeur inside. 'The Soviet people put them at my disposal day and night. I have lived through dreadful times and they have broken me. Remember, Jerzy: *nie warto*, it is not worth it. This is the harvest of compromise.'

Forty years on, in Holstebro, Grotowski talked to me of this moment as of a turning point in his life. Every time he thought about it he saw it as the opposite of the scene in which Satan tempted Christ. He asked himself if, without this situation and without these words, he would have been able to stand firm in Poland. Zavadsky had been his great master.

In 1976 while on a visit to Moscow Grotowski, now famous, was informed that Zavadsky was in hospital but had insisted on being taken home and was waiting for him there. From his sickbed he showed Grotowski the translations of *Towards a Poor Theatre* in different languages which he had had sent by the various Russian embassies. It was as though his life had regained a meaning through Grotowski's work. But when a nurse entered the room, Zavadsky immediately lowered his voice and changed the subject. Even so close to death, he was still afraid.

But that day in Opole in 1961 Grotowski and I kept well clear of personal confessions. All this was later revealed to me through the web of our relationship, which began at a table at the *Pająk*. That day at the restaurant, Grotowski and I talked of everything and nothing. We spoke of life *sub specie aeternitatis* and *sub specie praesentis*. We cannot escape from the spirit of the times, and yet we have to find an enduring value for our actions. We must act *sub specie aeternitatis* and, at the same time, behave *sub specie praesentis*, so that the reality surrounding us does not overwhelm us.

It was a long lunch, and that evening I took the train to Cracow. There had been just time enough to find out that we had some books in common and that we knew some unusual names, and already I was on my way. My life was full of such encounters.

In Warsaw I relapsed into a state of depression. Everything which had previously fascinated me about socialist Poland had now become a ground for criticism. The theatres were crowded because the workers were obliged to go there. The interest in poets whose books were selling like hot cakes was proof that freedom was only attainable through literary fiction. Privileges for artists were proof of the discrimination and the unjust conditions in which the workers lived. Poland was a prison, where you could neither have a passport nor travel abroad as could citizens in capitalist Europe. The secret police were omnipresent and the friendliness of a girl could conceal the interest of an informer.

The Christmas holidays arrived. I decided to spend them in Zakopane, a small town in the Tatra mountains which was the haunt of artists and intellectuals. I had to change trains at Cracow. At the bar of the Hotel Francuski I met Grotowski once again. I told him about my situation, my disenchantment with Poland, my lack of progress at the theatre school and the feeling of suffocation that never left me. How much vodka had we been drinking? What time of night was it? He proposed that I should go and work with him, straight away, in January. He was finishing one production, *Kordian*, and was about to start on another. I could be his assistant.

Why did he make that proposal? Perhaps because it brought prestige to have a foreigner in one's theatre. Why did I accept? Probably because by now I felt a lack of oxygen, I had nothing to lose, and my only alternative was to return to Norway without a director's diploma and without my political faith.

At a distance of nearly forty years, I now see how Grotowski, through theatre technique, always conducted his very personal research in a profound symbiotic relationship with another person. When I left Opole after a period of nearly three years, he embarked on this sort of relationship with Ryszard Cieślak. The result was extraordinary: *The Constant Prince*. So too was the incredible deepening of the training which was revealed to me during the seminars that Grotowski and Cieślak held at Odin Teatret each summer from 1966 to 1969. When Grotowski became involved in paratheatre in the seventies, his privileged companion became Jacek Zmysłowski whom I never met. He died in America of leukaemia in February 1982. When Grotowski spoke to me of him and of his death, his voice betrayed emotion. It is the only time I saw him with tears in his eyes. I believe that one of the motives for his close friendship with the American theatre director, André Gregory and his wife, Mercedes, who directed films, was their generous help, both human and financial, during the many months of Jacek's illness in America. Today it is Thomas Richards who has not only become Grotowski's privileged collaborator, but also his official heir.

From 1962 to 1964 I was this privileged companion.

In the beginning of January I announced to my teacher, Bohdan Korzeniewski, that I was leaving the school. I intended to take the exam as an external student by preparing a production in a theatre and submitting it to the judgement of the school commission. Korzeniewski looked at me, stupefied, when I told him I was going to Opole to the Teatr 13 Rzędów. I don't think he had ever seen one of Grotowski's performances. Behind his serious and ironical expression he must surely have thought that I was crazy, and that I would never be able to finish the school: I had a scholarship for only one year.

At the end of January 1962 I arrived in Opole.

Archetypes and Shamans
Grotowski was completing rehearsals of *Kordian* by Słowacki, a key text in Polish Romanticism. It is the story of an aristocrat who wants to liberate

his country by assassinating the Tsar. The attempt fails and Kordian is sent for examination to a psychiatric hospital. After being diagnosed as healthy, he is put to death.

Grotowski had transformed the text, setting the whole play in a psychiatric hospital. Kordian's patriotic tirades thus became the outbursts of a sick mind. The spectators were the patients, scattered around the room between beds on which the actors moved about, giving life to visions of madness. Zbigniew Cynkutis was Kordian. The tenderness aroused by his youthfulness and the melodious quality of his voice clashed constantly and surprisingly with his acrobatic vitality. The metal bunk-beds were perforated structures on which the actors climbed, assuming daring positions as if to display their frenzied ravings. This physical intensity gave the performance a suggestive force that I did not remember from *Dziady*.

As soon as I arrived Grotowski handed me a 24-page pamphlet entitled *Możliwość teatru* (The Possibility of Theatre), fresh from the printers and with his name on the cover. One half of it consisted of texts by Grotowski and Flaszen, and the other of extracts by Polish critics about Teatr 13 Rzędów's productions. Flaszen and Grotowski set out the main points of their vision: that the specific characteristic of theatre consists in the live and immediate contact between actor and spectator; for each production a new way of organising space has to be found, creating a unity and a physical osmosis which mingle actors and spectators, and favour contact; the performance originates from the contact between two *ensembles*, that of the actors and that of the spectators; the director has to 'direct' both these *ensembles*, consciously moulding their interaction in order to reach an archetype, and thereby the 'collective subconscious' of the two *ensembles*; these become aware of the archetype through a dialectic of apotheosis and derision which is applied to the text.

By now Grotowski had put aside avant-garde texts and was concentrating on the classics. He maintained that the classics contained certain archetypes and key situations from human destiny which were inherent in every culture; for example, contested love (Romeo and Juliet or Tristan and Isolde), or the individual who sacrifices himself for the group (Christ or Prometheus). The performance should be an act of collective introversion, a ceremony which would strip the mask from everyday life and confront the spectator with those situations that constitute the essence of individual and collective experience. In such performances, the actors had to be shamans who could reveal to the spectators the relationship between their own personal experience and the collective archetypes contained in the text. They had to be able to transform themselves under the gaze of the spectators, concentrating to the point of trance. As Grotowski told me shortly after my arrival in Opole, in the interview for *Sipario*: 'Actors must know how to assail their own "psychic humps" with conscious cruelty, and reach the inner layer from where they can attack the collective "psychic hump": the community's images, myths, archetypes and dreams. It befalls the director to stimulate this creative process in the actor in order to confront myth and society, and by profaning them both, to corroborate them both. The postulate of the actor is connected to the postulate of spiritual life. If God exists, He may have a spiritual life instead of us. But what if we maintain that he does not exist?'

In *Kordian* I saw abstract theory become flesh and blood: archetypes, the dialectic of apotheosis and derision, the direction of the two *ensembles*, all gave rise to a situation of heroism and abnegation with which I could identify. At the same time, a mocking irony was thrown in my face like a bucket of cold water, freezing my reactions. In the original text, in a long monologue, Kordian solemnly swears to give his own blood to save the country from the oppression of the Tsar. In the performance this moving speech was proffered by a man in a fit of delirium, stretched out on a bed while a doctor bled him in order to lower his blood pressure.

In *Kordian* there was no longer that arbitrariness which had seemed to me to characterise the actions of the actors in *Dziady*. I perceived a paradoxical logic which emphasised the text as though it were speaking of me and of the present. The way in which actors and spectators were distributed in space was profoundly coherent. I was full of admiration for the dramatic solutions, the interpretation of the text and the actors' performance.

The creator of the scenic space was Jerzy Gurawski, an architect (not a scenographer) of the same age as Grotowski. Their encounter belongs to the category of events that can well be described as historical. Neither one of them would have been capable of arriving at such extraordinary solutions without the other. Gurawski's contribution to *Kordian*, *Doctor Faustus* and *The Constant Prince* was exceptional. When his collaboration was lacking, Grotowski's scenic space was reduced to an empty room with the spectators seated at the sides, thus involuntarily becoming a theatre in the round. Gurawski was a modest man who was seldom to be seen at the theatre and who worked by himself while remaining in constant contact with Grotowski. In the case of *Doctor Faustus* too, where I was assistant director, he neither attended rehearsals nor intervened in the realisation of his designs. He was an unforgettable personality who, through his encounter with Grotowski, changed the conception of scenic space for

generations to come. Theatre history has not given him the prominence
he deserves, whereas Grotowski himself always underlined his importance. It is often the case that the creativity of a group, their collective
tension and effective symbiosis are associated with a single name.

Another outstanding personality was Ludwik Flaszen who was a few
years older than Grotowski. He was the theatre's literary director (in
Poland, every theatre had an artistic and a literary director and he had
filled this function at the reputable Slowacki Theatre in Cracow). He
played an invaluable role as an 'inside critic', a perpetual doubter and an
insistent 'devil's advocate'. Both Grotowski and Flaszen used to relate
laughingly how, one day in the spring of 1959, Flaszen had been sitting in
the journalist's club in Cracow wondering whether to accept an offer to
direct the Teatr 13 Rzędów. By chance he had seen Grotowski pass by and
it entered his mind to propose that he should be his co-director. What
amused them was the fact that Flaszen, in his capacity of theatre critic had
written a somewhat sceptical review of Grotowski's production of *Uncle
Vania* in March 1959, drawing attention to the lack of humour and excessive intellectuality of the director.

Behind this joking and self-ironical version, the truth is another.
Flaszen had had meetings with Grotowski to discuss the artistic
programme for their future theatre which was to be based on theatricality
and autonomy from literature. This pair, who barely knew each other and
had never collaborated before, left Cracow where they had their roots, for
Opole to direct a minute theatre which had opened in 1958 and whose
name derived from the thirteen rows of seats lined up in front of a tiny
stage[3].

It was a pleasure to listen to Flaszen. His conversation proceeded by
paradoxes, leaps from one idea to another, associations, *quid pro quos* and
puns. He did not express himself with Grotowski's fluency, but in staccato
phrases punctuated by pregnant pauses, and increasing in intensity as he
picked up the thread once again. He displayed nostalgia for the Emperor
Franz Josef of Austria for whom his father, a freight agent, had fought
during the First World War. His sense of humour could be ferocious and

---

[3] There was an 'artists' club' in Opole, where writers, architects, painters, designers, actors
and journalists met to chat and drink. It used to organise 'literary Thursdays', also inviting
outside artists. In 1958, Stanisław Łopuszańska and Eugeniusz Ławski, a couple of actors
who had previously worked at the Reduta Theatre and were then engaged by the Teatr Ziemi
Opolskiej - Opole's official theatre - transformed this club of eighty square metres, into the
Teatr 13 Rzędów (theatre of the 13 rows). Here they presented literary montages, poetry
evenings and plays. Among others, they invited the young student director, Jerzy Grotowski,
to direct a contemporary text by Jerzy Krzysztoń, *Pechowy* (The Unlucky).

irreverent. One of the first times we lunched together in Opole, I was telling - shocked and upset - about my recent visit to Auschwitz, when he interrupted me to ask point-blank if I knew who had built Auschwitz. I had difficulty in understanding what he meant. It was obvious: the Nazis. Flaszen shook his head: 'No, it was the Jews.' And both he and Grotowski burst out laughing at my bewilderment.

Flaszen was a master of the art of dense writing. In the programmes of the Teatr 13 Rzędów it was he who formulated the conception which characterised the work. It was Flaszen (in an article on *Akropolis* in 1962) who spoke of 'poor theatre', organised on the principle of the strictest autarchy where 'it is absolutely forbidden to introduce into the play anything which is not already there at the very beginning. A certain number of people and objects are gathered in the theatre. They must be sufficient to handle any of the play's situations[4]. 'Poor theatre' was a perfect definition to describe the work process in *Akropolis*. Grotowski took it up again in 1965 in his article *Towards a Poor Theatre* and made it into a slogan, a battle cry to which he gave quite another meaning: 'Theatre can exist without make-up, without costumes and scenography, without a separate performance area (stage), without sound effects and lighting, etc. It cannot exist without the actor-spectator relationship of perceptual, direct, "live" communion[5].

And yet the costumes, props and above all the organisation of the space were very sophisticated and relatively costly at the Teatr 13 Rzędów. Suffice it to recall the scenic installation for *Doctor Faustus* or *The Constant Prince* which was a theatre within a theatre, with Waldemar Krygier's costumes stirring up discordant associations; or the emotive effectiveness of József Szajna's costumes and his metallic tubes which invaded the space in *Akropolis*, evoking the feverish and exhausting work in the extermination camps.

To do 'poor theatre' you have to be rich. But Grotowski's wealth was not money. It was the creative resources of the ensemble: of the architect Gurawski; of Flaszen, the devil's advocate; of Krygier and Szajna, the creators of costumes which were bewitching emblems; of Grotowski himself who tore the classics to pieces in search of archetypes. And then there were the actors: Rena Mirecka, Zygmunt Molik, Zbigniew Cynkutis,

[4] See Ludwik Flaszen, *Akropolis di Wyspiański* in Eugenio Barba's *Alla ricerca del teatro perduto*, Marsilio, Padua 1965 p.166 and also *Akropolis: treatment of the text* in Jerzy Grotowski's *Towards a Poor Theatre*, Odin Teatrets Forlag, Holstebro 1968, p.61.
[5] Jerzy Grotowski, 'Ku teatrowi ubogiemu', *Odra*, No.9, Wrocław 1965 and also *Towards a Poor Theatre*, cit. p.18.

Antoni Jahołkowski and Ryszard Cieślak. Their voices and gestures fill my senses when I visit them in my memory. The performance is something that happened between them and me and the consequences live on, are transmitted, become embodied in new life.

Grotowski was right in taking up Flaszen's expression 'poor theatre' and making it into the battle cry of an ideal theatre which he and his actors incarnated. The craftsman-like discipline, the rigour of the composition, the artificiality and the technical sagacity were the conditions necessary to trigger in the actor a process so deep that it led to a 'total act'. 'The actors, like the figures in El Greco's paintings, are able to radiate light by way of a personal technique, becoming sources of "spiritual light".' This statement by Grotowski in *Towards a Poor Theatre* (p.20) is by no means a metaphor. It is a pure statement of fact.

There were eight actors when I arrived in Opole. Zygmunt Molik, Rena Mirecka and Antoni Jahołkowski had been with Grotowski and Flaszen from the beginning; Andrzej Bielski, Ewa Lubowiecka and Zbigniew Cynkutis from 1960. Maja Komorowska, a cousin of Grotowski (who later became a well known film actress), and Ryszard Cieślak arrived at the start of the 1961-62 season. Only Molik, Mirecka and Cynkutis had finished the theatre school. Maja Komorowska and Ryszard Cieślak had completed the school for puppeteers and all the others (including Stanisław Scierski who arrived in 1964) had experience of student theatre and received the actor's diploma by passing an exam after several years at the Teatr 13 Rzędów.

I arrived at a theatre which was neither a 'group' theatre nor a rebellious one. It began as a small and traditional provincial theatre with a mixed bunch of actors and with an artistic and a literary director who barely knew one another. The actors were not extraordinary personalities, but having moved to the provinces, they simply expected important roles. There were not many new candidates after the first few productions, apart from Ryszard Cieślak who, as he later told me, decided to go to Opole after seeing a performance of *Shakuntala*. The Teatr 13 Rzędów contained, on a smaller scale, all the hierarchies and specialisation of the larger theatres. There were technicians, administrators, secretaries and even a wardrobe mistress who helped the actors to dress and took care of the costumes after the performance. About fifteen people in all.

The transformation of this provincial theatre into an ensemble, whose artistic intransigence would sow the seeds of a profound regeneration of our art, is one of the most emblematic episodes of our century. It involved the rediscovery and the practice of training, innovations in scenic space, the actor-spectator relationship, the dramaturgical restructuring of the text, the sense and the value of theatre in our society. All these questions and practical solutions were to inspire the new generation, and more especially the theatrical mutation constituted by groups that would spring up outside institutional theatre at the end of the sixties. The evolution of the Teatr 13 Rzędów into a Teatr-Laboratorium is an example of a shabby little theatre which starts out as literary-artistic avant-garde and ends by embodying a creative process which is the unfolding of an artistic, political and spiritual attitude. A theatrical palingenesis which lasted ten years.

The fate of these actors has always moved me. Through the discipline to which they submitted themselves, the risk of political anathema and Grotowski's inflexibility, they managed to become the living symbol of a theatre which yearned to transcend itself. Then they renounced their identity as actors and as artists who encounter spectators. When Grotowski decided in 1970 not to do any more productions, most of his actors followed their director along his new path. They became pedagogues, experts in paratheatre, guides in whom both young and old placed their trust, and only seldom trod the boards again[6].

I have never been able to escape a feeling of sadness each time I met one of Grotowski's actors, especially Cieślak. I could never explain the sensation which assailed me when I bumped into these actors who were rooted in my memory through the radiant characters they had played, the unforgettable sonority of their voices, the expressions on their faces and the power and vulnerability of their gestures or their ecstatic immobility. I admired their stalwart autonomy, but the solitude which appeared to me to engulf them brought a lump to my throat. Their camping outside the normal boundaries of theatre was not of their own choosing but was the consequence of another's need which they had, nonetheless, willingly taken upon themselves. Only in 1996 did I succeed in giving a name to this sensation of mine. During a session of the University of Eurasian Theatre in Scilla, a director who was about forty years old told of the breaking up of the group he had been leading for more than ten years. "I lived through three years of mourning – he said – before I could go back to work again."

'Mourning' is the term I associate with Grotowski's actors. I recall my

---

[6] Ryszard Cieślak, for example, acted in Peter Brook's *Mahabharata* (1985-1988). Some say that his portrayal of the blind king was extraordinary. I haven't seen it, but people close to me told me how much he had suffered during the rehearsals after so many years away from the stage. It is enough to read the merciless interview with Andrzej Seweryn, his Polish fellow actor in Brook's production, in *Notatnik Teatralny*, No. 10, Wrocław 1995.

mother who lost her husband at the age of thirty-three. She could laugh, enjoy herself, talk or flirt with other men. But in the darkest corner of her heart lurked the awareness of an irreplaceable loss or of an irrevocable liberation, the memory of being struck by lightning and surviving while the house in which you grew up is reduced to ashes.

Crossing Deserts and Hitchhiking

As I said before, Grotowski was twenty-eight, barely three years older than me, but I considered him my master from the day I decided to interrupt my studies at the theatre school in Warsaw to follow his work.

From the very start we began to identify ourselves with two different roles which were emphasised by the nicknames we gave each other. He was the old Lama and I was the adolescent Kim from Kipling's novel. He was the speculative Faustus, and I the vitalist Don Juan. He was the introvert Ramakrishna, and I the extrovert Vivekananda. Yet Grotowski had been an actor, had published articles in various newspapers, had been a leading exponent of the political youth movement, as well as lecturer in Indian and Chinese philosophy and assistant at the Cracow theatre school. But he aroused in me an unexplainable protective instinct. He had constant health problems, mainly with his kidneys. He seemed to me to be rather inexperienced and even provincial. I had had a thousand jobs in a thousand different places, as a sailor I had been on long trips to the East, and had lived as a vagabond, wandering through Greece, Lapland, Turkey and Israel.

At the time Grotowski spoke no foreign languages except for Russian, and I often used to translate texts for him. I was indignant and felt sorry for him over the injustice of which he was a victim through the ban against free travel. In those days, in socialist Poland, it was impossible to get a passport and acquire foreign currency. You could only go abroad if you had a scholarship, as a member of an official delegation or on the formal invitation of someone who guaranteed to cover the cost of your travel and stay.

An artist knows many things, but is aware of them only at the end of the work. At that point Grotowski was just starting out. His 'knowledge' was in an embryo state and was not noticed as was the case from 1966 on when, almost from one day to the next, he was recognised as a great master. He was neither well known nor particularly appreciated in Polish theatre circles. So why did I stop in Opole?

I would be lying if I claimed to have been thunderstruck by *Dziady* – the first production by the Teatr 13 Rzędów that I ever saw – or seduced

33

on the spot by Grotowski's theories, by his direction of the actors and the spectators or by the dialectic of apotheosis and derision. I was by no means aware of participating in a theatre revolution and following a conquistador in an artistic adventure. I would be cheating if I were to say today that Grotowski made me discover that the theatre craft is grafted on to something you have in your blood and not just something you think with your brain.

My role as 'assistant director' in *Akropolis* and *Doctor Faustus* consisted in sitting and watching the progress of rehearsals and training sessions and then, sitting alone with Grotowski, making comments, expressing doubts, asking for explanations, making suggestions, opening up for all my associations, impressions and questions. This I did for thirty months. Only rarely did I have the opportunity to direct the actors myself. When this happened it was always a painful experience. The actors followed my suggestions with an ironical smile that was more or less evident, and I felt paralysed by the banality of my instructions. During rehearsals I was an immobile yet attentive and receptive being who never actively intervened in the work process.

During the rehearsals for *Akropolis* I watched Jósef Szajna with his shirtsleeves rolled up over his Auschwitz tattoo, disembowelling coarse sacks only to sew them together again, and making holes in them which he then covered with patches: and there were the costumes whose cruel and mocking 'poverty' imprisoned and dehumanised the actions of the performers. I keenly observed the actors while they were busy with a pile of metal tubes which they carried around, hanging them above my head, nailing them to the floor in front of my feet, using them as beds, shelters, even as spouses. For the space of a few minutes those situations were like bursts of thunder and lightning. Then repetition took over and they became tedious. Is this the way to become a director? Glued to my chair, I asked myself what I was learning.

Today I might reply that I learnt how there is action in waiting and waiting in action, how the difference between waiting and action in life exists only for the blind and, in the theatre, only for the hurried spectator. I learnt to 'see', to penetrate beyond the surface, to look, in order to reach the depths, to concentrate on recognising the essential and distinguishing the superfluous from the necessary. I believed one had to collaborate with Providence; but Providence is not only that which saves you from the shipwreck in which everyone else perishes. It is also that which saves the others, while snatching away the plank you are clinging to, leaving you to drown in a watery desert. I consoled myself saying: *tu l'as voulu George*

Dandin ... You must remain loyal to your decision, stay with it to its ultimate consequence, follow it wherever it leads you. I thought of Lao Tse, the old man-child who allowed a black buffalo to guide him in his wanderings. But this wise and poetic image did not comfort me.

It was a true crossing of the desert. A technique exists for surviving the hours that seem eternal, for fighting against the monotony and the sluggishness of footsteps one after another along a route that seems to take you nowhere, in order to resist the voice of temptation that constantly whispers: it is not worth going on. It is impossible to cross the desert if you think only of yourself. You must project the whole of your mind, your will, your passion towards another person. In *Vol de nuit* Saint-Exupéry describes his wanderings in the Egyptian desert after his plane has crashed. It was as though, obsessively, in his thoughts, he embraced his friend Henri Guillaumet, one of the heroes of Aéropostale who, after crashing in the Andes, had walked for five days and nights, fighting against the desire to give up and lie down in the snow. Guillaumet had managed to survive by keeping his thoughts fixed on his wife, who would not have received a pension if he had disappeared and his body had not been found. It is possible to cross the desert only if your concentration is 'elsewhere', with someone else, and you become insensible to weather conditions, exhaustion, the intolerance of the body and the doubts of the mind.

For me, this 'elsewhere' was the incipient bond with Grotowski, this friend of my own age who was both vulnerable and yet so strong. It was a bond in which tenderness and the impulse to protect him were reinforced by an affinity which, day by day, brought us closer together.

The days passed, and with them I saw the certainty fade that what I was participating in might serve me in my future career as a director. The theatre in which I had become involved really was like the critics, the majority of theatre people and the political authorities described it: bizarre, formalist and without any artistic and social resonance. Objectively, the facts proved them right: the spectators were few, often very few, sometimes non-existent.

I myself did not understand everything that happened in the work. But sometimes, in *Akropolis*, while watching a scene with its contrasting rhythms or its cruel details, my vision became double and an invisible veil of tears turned my gaze inwards, towards a secret and unknown part of me. That scene, its intonations and its movements were gusts of the wind of Pan which stirred my senses. I heard voices, I answered them, and while I was lost in this dialogue, the performance was no longer there. I was in its centre and I had gone beyond its limits, I was somewhere else. But where?

I crossed the desert and unwittingly absorbed the conviction that the theatre is a flame needing wood – the body and soul of the actor – in order to burn. In that expanse of sand, I suddenly saw the burning bush. For a fraction of a second the flame sprang from the actor, illuminating a hidden part of me. It spoke, became *mythos-soma*, shook me and led me along a shadowy path, holding my hand and helping me to overcome my hesitations and fears.

With the arrival of summer, the holidays interrupted rehearsals of *Akropolis*. Grotowski had been chosen to be a member of the Polish delegation to the Youth Festival in Helsinki. They were to travel on the liner *Batory* which would also house them during the Festival[7]. Grotowski and I agreed to meet in Finland to spread information about the Teatr 13 Rzędów to the newspapers and in theatrical circles.

I hitchhiked to Finland where I stayed with Lars Biström, a journalist with Finnish television whom I knew from Oslo. He immediately agreed to interview Grotowski, to organise a press conference and to present him to theatre people. We used his house as a base. One evening Lars invited us to a dinner of lobster: these archaic shellfish – he said – should provoke archetypical resonances in us and the antithesis between their hard outer shell and the tender flesh should dialectically reinvigorate our capacity for apotheosis and derision.

His stay in Finland had incalculable consequences for Grotowski. There he met Raymonde and Valentin Temkine who played a decisive role in making him known abroad. Raymonde was a theatre critic in Paris, writing for *Combat*, the newspaper founded by Camus, as well as for other French and Swiss magazines. They met Grotowski on a bus trip to Tampere to visit a modern open-air theatre. At Easter 1963 the Temkines came to Opole and saw *Akropolis*. From that moment they became tenacious and generous supporters, doing their utmost for Grotowski and his theatre and offering hospitality in their flat in Paris to whoever of us passed through. Raymonde Temkine wrote innumerable articles on the theatre and the visions of Grotowski, and in 1968 she crowned her work by publishing her book *Grotowski*[8]. The tour of the Teatr-Laboratorium 13 Rzędów to Paris in 1966 was prepared by this tireless woman who, through her writings and her contacts, succeeded in opening many doors.

---

[7] A festival organised regularly by the socialist countries. This was the first time it took place outside the 'iron curtain' countries.

[8] La Cité, Lausanne 1968, published in Italian the following year by De Donato.

She took a stand and fought for it to the bitter end.

Back in Warsaw at the beginning of August, Grotowski and I celebrated in advance his twenty-ninth birthday in the bar of the Hotel Bristol. A couple of days later he left for China for three weeks, once again with an official delegation. I, on the other hand, through the Ministry of Culture, had been engaged by a Bulgarian circus touring Poland. During the course of three weeks we gave thirty-two performances in Częstochowa, Opole, and Kłodzko in a tent packed with over two thousand five hundred spectators. I was impressed by the harsh life of the artists, whose very survival literally depended on the effectiveness of many hours of daily training. Afterwards I wrote a report for the Ministry in which my comments and reflections were coloured by Grotowski's theatrical vision. I spoke of 'shamans' and 'supernatural' actions; of the *soma* – the body – as efficiency, vigour and perfection; of psychic factors such as the excitement and euphoria of the audience; of the dramatic quality of the dangerous acts; of the elementary theatricality emphasised through music, lights and the rolling of the drums; of the spectator who was aware that the following act would be different but with the same incisive dynamics; of the absence of scenography and other superfluous elements; of the alternating relationships with the audience – aristocratic and distant for the trapeze artists, informal and burlesque for the clowns; of the masterly succession of the acts with their resulting impact on the spectators. There was no doubt about the pertinence of Eisenstein's observations concerning the 'montage of attractions'.

In mid-September I was back in Opole. Grotowski recounted his Chinese expedition and I my experiences with the Bulgarian circus. Rehearsals of *Akropolis* were in the final stages. With the first public performance at the beginning of October, I felt something that was emotion and yet at the same time a sense of unreality. I saw again the days and the hours; I recalled, nail by nail, the monotony of the construction, and now I too was drifting away on board a small boat. I thought of the dedication that Grotowski had written in the programme for *Kordian*, welcoming me to his theatre: 'To Eugenio who is preparing for the struggle, as a good beginning to an arduous and wearisome adventure in the craft'.

I opened the *Akropolis* programme and reread, as though it were a prayer, the text by Tadeusz Borowski, a Polish writer who had been in Auschwitz and had committed suicide after the liberation:

We work underground and in the fields, sheltered by a roof and under the rain, with shovels, carts, pickaxes, sledgehammers. We carry sacks of cement, we pile up bricks, we lay railway tracks, we put up fences, we trample the earth. We are building the foundations of a new civilisation. Only now do I recognise the price of antiquity. What will the world know about us if the Germans win? Gigantic buildings, motorways and factories are shooting up, and monuments reach up into the clouds. They are killing our families, the sick, the old. They are murdering the children. And no one will know anything about us. Our voices are suffocated by the cries of poets, lawyers, philosophers and princes. They are creating beauty, goodness, truth. They are creating a religion.

(...) Once we were returning to the camp. An orchestra was accompanying the marching of the prisoners. Dozens of other squads arrived and waited in front of the gate: tens of thousands of men. And then, lorries loaded with naked women appeared. They were stretching out their arms and shouting: 'Save us. They are taking us to the gas. Save us'. And they passed by close to us, tens of thousands of men in total silence. No one moved; not a hand was raised. Because before the dead, the living are always right.

The Theatre's New Testament

Today, when speaking about Grotowski, one usually thinks of the expression 'poor theatre' and of a performance based essentially on the encounter between actor and spectator without the aid of other artistic disciplines such as scenography, music or literature. His subversive action is thus reduced to Lope de Vega's 'three tables, two people and one passion'. This way of thinking cripples our century's most wide-reaching revolution which has changed the material body of the theatre in four fundamental areas: the relationship between stage and auditorium; the relationship between the director and the text; the function of the actor; and the transgressive possibilities of the theatre craft.

It was Richard Wagner who first created an emotive integration between the stage and the audience in Bayreuth by immersing both stage and auditorium in darkness. By preventing the spectators from seeing and distracting one another, he had drawn them into the magic circle of the action on stage. This integration was developed in depth by Stanislavsky, who concentrated on the work of the actor whose 'sincerity' had to engage the spectator emotionally.

By abolishing the physical separation between actor and spectator, Grotowski realised to the letter the unity between stage and audience. It was a Copernican revolution with unpredictable consequences for the dramaturgy of the production, for the performance of the actors and for the perception of the spectators. The abolition of these two distinct spaces

- the stage for the actors and the auditorium for the spectators – corresponds to the abolition of the bars in the lions' cage at the zoo. Protected by the bars, we can stand a few centimetres away from the king of the animals and yet feel safe. Take away the 'bars' in the performance and our feeling of security vanishes so that participation acquires quite another intensity. Today this osmosis has become a 'commonplace', both in traditional and street theatre, and it is difficult to imagine the shock and impact produced at the beginning of the sixties by productions like *Akropolis*, *Doctor Faustus* and *The Constant Prince* or by the ideas which inspired them and the way they were created.

The director's intervention in the text is not new in our century. It had taken place either through a particular interpretation which completely transformed the work without even changing a single word (as was the case, sometimes, with Stanislavsky), or by means of a 'restructuring' of the text (as in Meyerhold's *The Government Inspector* by Gogol). Grotowski, however, approached the classics with the stubborn conviction that they contained an archetype, a situation which was fundamental to the human condition. To make the spectator aware of this, he constructed scenic equivalents which derived in a coherent manner from the text but altered its form with an extremism previously unknown in the history of theatre and which at the time was considered to be sacrilege. Such a process generated a new *avatar* of the text which thus acquired the same function as the myth that the Greek tragedians in Athens interpreted with a total freedom like a matrix of variants (for example, Antigone dies in Sophocles yet, in Euripides, she survives and marries Hemon, son of Creon).

Grotowski started the tradition of the director who dissects and operates in a drastic way on the literary structure. His aim was not only to present texts in contemporary terms, but above all to recreate through them the experience of extreme historical events as well as individual and collective obsessions. His attraction towards the classics and his sincere faith in their value were revealed through blasphemy and profanation[9] .

This dramaturgical method of paring down the text in order to liberate the archetypical soul was embodied in actors whose technical quality became unique to the theatre of that period. There was a tradition of mime in Poland with Henryk Tomaszewski, and there were imaginative student

---

[9] This treatment scandalised many theatre artists, as for example the French director Roger Planchon, and above all the critics. Raymonde Temkine, who was so totally convinced by the work of Grotowski, is touching in her sincerity when she admits having 'to do violence to herself and go beyond the taboos inherited from a university education', *Grotowski*, La Cité, Lausanne 1968, p. 87.

theatres whose style broke with the 'verisimilitude' of the official stages. There were also traditional theatres where, thanks to the playwrights (Ionesco, Beckett, Różewicz, Mrożek), scenographers (Szajna or Kantor) or directors (Skuszanka, Swinarski) the acting possessed a refined theatricality.

But Grotowski pursued the vision of an actor capable of creating 'signs', true visible, auditory and above all psychic shocks for the spectator and for the collective imagination. The search for these 'signs' whose dynamism is imbued with associations is not based on psychology or the mechanics of cause and effect, but on a theatrical logic. This logic is rooted in organic coherence and presupposes a physical and psychic discipline, in other words a technique. The mastery over this technique becomes a personal process which makes actors discover their own interior flora and fauna, introducing them to the shared territory of the collective imagination. According to the formula of Stanislavsky, the training and the work on the performance become essentially the work of the actor on him/herself, also as an individual. This dialectic – the text stripped of its flesh and the actor who incarnates the spirit of the text – is not an abstract theory or a vision-mirage, but a technical discipline, a succession of concrete exercises and actions that are described in detail[10].

Today one can admire Grotowski's open-mindedness and his loyalty towards the creative process. This attitude helped him to discover new perspectives and to explore without being held back by his own theories and preconceptions. A telling example of this was the training. It had started out as a way of resolving the concrete problems of some of the actors during the rehearsals of *Akropolis*, but Grotowski let it develop to the extent of becoming an autonomous activity which was not necessarily linked to the preparation of a production.

There is a constant and complementary double aspect to Grotowski's theatre work. On the one hand the performance is a 'lay' ritual, enveloping actors and spectators in a special osmosis and making them meditate on the wounds of the human condition. The references to and the examples of this conception relate to the history of the theatre and to the protagonists of the *Wielka Reforma*, the Great Reform, as the Poles call the period of ferment and subversion that began with Antoine, Stanislavsky and Reinhardt and ended in the thirties with Nazism and Stalinism.

On the other hand, there is a secret tension going beyond the artistic

[10] See Eugenio Barba, *Expériences du théâtre laboratoire 13 Rzędów*, Opole 1962; *Alla ricerca del teatro perduto*, Marsilio, Padua 1965; Jerzy Grotowski, *Towards a Poor Theatre*, Odin Teatrets Forlag, Holstebro 1968.

and social value of the performance towards a religiosity (not a religion) which, for as long as I have known Grotowski, has been connected above all to Hinduism. It is this tension which, through aesthetics and technique, has pushed him towards transgression, a key word in Grotowski's terminology during the Opole years. The performance is an act of transgression that allows us to break down our barriers, transcend our limits, fill our emptiness, fulfil ourselves, enter into the territory of the *sacrum*. Actors provoke and challenge themselves and the spectators, profaning images, sentiments and generally accepted opinions. This desecration of taboos causes a shock, shatters the mask imposed by historical and biographical circumstances, denudes us. Grotowski's transgression was applied to the values of the tradition handed down to us through classical texts, to ways of conceiving and practising theatre and to the conception of a utilitarian or supinely ideological art.

Such an attitude was insidiously subversive in a socialist regime. The authorities soon realised that this was not a formalist theatre but a 'nucleus of strength' rising up in the midst of their manipulated world and rejecting it. It was a symbolic rejection, the only weapon available to the artist. It was disheartening during those years to read and listen to the accusations of the 'committed' artists who charged Grotowski with being non-political. This sort of attitude revealed a total blindness to the rebellious extremism of his way of thinking and of his theatre practice, not to mention his struggle and strategy to defend his own truth without self-betrayal, and without letting himself be crushed.

With this particular vision of theatre and his technical capacity to implement it, Grotowski gave life to half a dozen productions. These created a resonance, made up of misunderstandings, passions, bewilderment and misinterpretation, but were only seen by a small number of spectators. Only *Akropolis*, *The Constant Prince* and, after 1971, *Apocalypsis cum figuris* travelled abroad. The disruptive force of Grotowski's ideas came mainly from his book *Towards a Poor Theatre* which was published in English in 1968, and from the mass of articles and essays which spread the legend of his Laboratorium everywhere. At the end of the sixties the revolution represented by the New Testament of the Theatre had inspired innumerable ways of imagining new theatre possibilities and a variety of practices to realise them. For this very reason its expansion was absorbed ever more into the omnipresent body of the Old Testament of the Theatre. Its example of subversion, courage and intransigence was transformed into an aesthetic category, or an example of technique cut off from its roots, which consisted in a need for transgression and a thirst for transcendence.

41

One of Grotowski's reasons for ceasing to do theatre was the fact that theatrical performance no longer satisfied his need for transgression. His subsequent activities continue to draw on the technique of the actor but above all they permit the discovery of other outlets for his tension towards the *sacrum*. Thus he keeps alive the provocation and transgression in relation to himself and also to those of us who observe him from the field of theatre, seeking to understand whether his actions still have a significance for us, for our craft and for the professional legacy to be handed down.

Relationships and Chess Games

I am trying to explain the origin of my bond with Grotowski and my persistence in remaining thirty long months in Opole. However, I don't want to create any misconceptions, as of a miracle happening there every day, or a permanent intoxication of the senses and the spirit. No, life there was monotonous and dull. The small town of sixty thousand inhabitants was grey, its cultural life was far from stimulating and, with rare exceptions, it was indifferent, if not hostile, to the Teatr 13 Rzędów. The work followed the same rhythm as any traditional Polish theatre: rehearsals from 10a.m. to 2p.m. and then a performance in the evening. During periods when there was no performance, there might be rehearsals in the evenings and these could well go on late into the night. There was a certain flexibility which was dictated by circumstance.

A rigid hierarchical structure separated artists from technical and administrative staff. Relationships were characterised by a rather formal courteousness which was typically Polish and demanded a polite form of address in the third person (equivalent to 'vous' in French), using the appellation *Pan* and *Pani* (Mr. and Ms.). Grotowski addressed the actors and me like this, and we did the same between ourselves and to him. Only Grotowski, Flaszen and Molik used the familiar form of 'you' to each other. The members of the theatre did not see much of each other outside work. We might go and have a drink together, and on rare occasions we would meet at the home of one of the married actors, eating and drinking until late, Flaszen and Grotowski included. On May 1st the whole theatre, led by Flaszen and Grotowski, participated in the procession of blue- and white-collar workers carrying huge placards promising to increase production and filing past the platform where the local communist party bosses stood smiling and waving.

During work the tone was one of polite correctness. I have never seen Grotowski irritated with his actors, and if he was, he was able to control himself. When I arrived, the actors were already used to looking for theatrical solutions, physical or vocal 'signs' which could unveil an archetype. This term was never used, but a word which often recurred was 'composition': the way in which the actors rendered their actions theatrical and concentrated. All the actors were patient, submitting themselves to continuous repetitions of the same scene or of short fragments. The atmosphere was one of craftsmen intent on the job in hand and speaking only when necessary.

All the actors were present at rehearsals, even when they did not all need to be there. It was in *Doctor Faustus* that Grotowski began working individually, with one actor at a time. One of the longest sessions lasting an entire night was with Ryszard Cieślak, and I remember it because it resulted in a double shock for me. During that period (February-March 1963) I was preparing a production based on Dante's *La Divina Commedia* which Grotowski had agreed should be presented as a part of the Teatr 13 Rzędów's repertoire[11].

This was the production that I planned to present to the Warsaw theatre school for my diploma[12]. As scenographer I had enlisted Roland Grünberg, a French graphic artist with a scholarship at the Cracow School of Art[13]. I intended to reconstruct a traditional stage on which scenes from

---

[11] The choice of *La Divina Commedia* was ideal for the Opole theatre's classical repertoire and Grotowski's theories. The journey theme made it possible to present an archetype and, as an Italian, it was appropriate that I choose a classic from my own culture. Grotowski and I discussed who might be the scenographer. I would have liked it to be Szajna, but he had already collaborated in *Akropolis* and it was better to find someone else. The name of Tadeusz Kantor came up. He was a painter, who occasionally directed plays by Witkacy (a couple of which I had seen in Cracow), but above all he was well known as a scenographer. He detested Grotowski and had often spoken of him in a very derogative way. It would have been a good move to bring him into our circle of acquaintances. So I arranged a meeting one morning with Kantor in a café in Cracow. I told him I was Italian, had a scholarship and was preparing a production of Dante, explaining some of my ideas. He seemed interested and began asking questions. Things appeared to be going well. Then he asked me where I planned to present it. 'In Opole', I replied. 'At the Teatr Ziemi Opolskiej?' he inquired. This was a traditional and mediocre repertory theatre. 'No', I said, 'at Grotowski's Teatr-Laboratorium.' Kantor gave me a withering look, got up and left without a word. I was never to meet him again.

[12] The production did not become a reality because, from what Grotowski told me, the authorities never gave their permission.

[13] Roland Grünberg and I were friends long before I went to Opole and I immediately thought of him after the incident with Kantor. I had also asked Roland to write the article on the Teatr 13 Rzędów for *Sipario*. I could not have allowed myself an enthusiastic tone since I was editing the issue. Roland was from Nancy and knew Jack Lang, the young director of the Student Theatre Festival. Back in Nancy, he managed to have Grotowski invited as a member of the festival jury in 1964. Roland also collaborated with me in creating the poster for *Ornitofilene*, Odin Teatret's first production in Oslo.

Oedipus Rex, Romeo and Juliet and Chekhov's *Three Sisters* would be played one after another as examples of the best European tradition. Every gesture, every tone, every invention would have communicated some particularity in the text, or a way of interpreting it and commenting on it. I had planned the auditorium as an empty space, rather like an Elizabethan theatre, with the spectators standing on platforms at different levels. Dante and his mother, as a family in flight, would move around, hiding underneath the platforms or suddenly overturning them, and all the while whispering, singing, negating Dante's text, and always in counterpoint with what was happening on stage. In the production that I had imagined, the great tradition of theatre would have continued imperturbably to present its masterpieces, while the world would be falling apart, under the feet of the same spectators.

I had spoken of all my ideas to Grotowski and he had approved them. Then after working a whole night with Grotowski, Cieślak gave life to Benvoglio's mad scene where he literally dismantled the two long tables at which the spectators of *Doctor Faustus* were supposed to sit. What had appeared at the start to be the last supper to which Faustus had invited his friends – the spectators – became in a few seconds an infernal bedlam of yells and destruction brought about by the furious courtier who was miraculously appeased by Faustus.

I waved goodbye to my idea of the *Divina Commedia* as a disruption of the entire scenic space. I reproached Grotowski his theft and he replied with an innocent air that it had been Cieślak who, during the night's work, had set about smashing the decor during an improvisation. I then told him of an episode that I had read in a book by André Salmon: at the beginning of the cubist period, whenever Braque saw Picasso approaching his atelier, he turned all the canvases he was working on to face the wall so that they could not be seen.

But during that rehearsal I had received another shock: the quality of Cieślak's performance, his state of fury, and the exceptional sang-froid and precision with which he made those heavy tables leap into the air only a few centimetres from the spectators' faces.

The serious and polite affability which characterised Grotowski during the work vanished after he became famous. I noticed it immediately when watching him direct Scandinavian actors during the first seminar organised with him at Odin Teatret in Holstebro in July 1966. He had become hard, impatient and could become irritated by a question which he considered silly, scolding his poor questioner in a harsh manner. When he was guiding someone in an improvisation or an exercise, that rigour became encouragement which stimulated the actor to overcome hesitation, conditioned reflexes, insecurity, and then the results achieved were unforgettable. But intransigent and severe behaviour had become a part of his *persona*, his way of presenting himself. Some people were fascinated by this inflexibility, while to others it appeared egocentric and rude. It was only in the nineties that age and probably physical weakness revealed, also in public, the gentle irony and warm tone that had always characterised him when he spoke to a person in private or in a small group.

In Opole, Grotowski's capacity to open up and be totally sincere with me was my most effective 'school of war' and the best lesson in understanding how to play chess with the powerful authorities *sub specie praesentis*: censorship, informers, secret police, politicians, critics and adversaries. Grotowski explained to me in the minutest detail how he intended to behave, what the probable and differing reactions would be, with whom and to what extent he could play on Polish patriotism in order to be 'ideologically incorrect' without creating problems at a high level with the Russians. I was a witness to the birth and development of those mental processes in him which turned into strategic moves to defend what is the 'essential'.

Terminology was important. Every word had to reflect the Word yet avoid being accused and condemned as 'idealistic' or 'mystical'. In socialist Poland you could be religious, openly profess your religion and frequent the omnipresent churches. The regime had succeeded in finding a *modus vivendi* with the powerful Catholic Church, and intellectuals and Catholic writers published one of the best magazines. But to be defined a 'mystic' or an 'idealist' meant that the regime considered you to be an opponent.

This incessant and cautious concentration on how to defend the 'firm', the 'hermitage' – as Grotowski used to call his theatre – brought about the transformation from Teatr 13 Rzędów to Teatr-Laboratorium 13 Rzędów. This simple change of name had unforeseeable consequences. In January 1962 the Polish Ministry of Culture sent forms round to every theatre inquiring which genre they practised: dramatic, musical, for children, puppet theatre, opera, operetta, laboratory, etc. Grotowski indicated the last of these since none of the others applied to the 13 Rzędów. He immediately realised the value of the term: it allowed him to justify research into what was 'essential' in theatre craft, the lengthy process involved in the preparation of a production, and the restricted number of spectators. What is more, the term made reference to a historical precedent, to the laboratories of Stanislavsky, the artist who was a model for Soviet theatre and therefore, like it or not, for the entire socialist block.

Without hesitating, Grotowski ordered some new headed writing paper, and very large letters on the programme for his new production, *Akropolis*, in October 1962 boldly announced: TEATR-LABORATORIUM 13 RZĘDÓW.

A Thousand and One Nights

Ever since my arrival in Opole it had been the custom for me and Grotowski to meet after work. I do not know how the actors reacted to this. They were always polite with me and some of them were even affectionate. Only Flaszen, though always friendly, appeared sceptical towards me and with his usual irony hinted that he could not understand why Grotowski talked to me so much[14].

Grotowski was certainly no gourmet. One of his greatest pleasures was eating tinned sardines. These were not to be found in the state food shops in Poland, so I brought them back from my travels abroad. He lived frugally, often eating in the Mleczny Bars, a chain of cheap restaurants of the capitalist fast food type. The food was tasteless and colourless, and you ate standing up as there were only a few tables and these were always occupied or covered in dirty plates.

He rented a small room where you could hardly reach the unmade bed for the piles of books surrounding it. It was as though he did not care where or how he lived, and this indifference has always characterised his living quarters. The successive places in which I visited him - the two small rooms at Irvine in California, or the minute apartment in Pontedera in Italy - although less untidy and choked by books, were bare and unadorned, and not the least attempt had been made to give a homely atmosphere to the place which is one's tent and refuge.

I had managed to rent a large comfortable room from a family of German origin, where I arranged all the books I had brought with me from Warsaw. I had a small gramophone and many records that I had bought in Poland - Jewish religious hymns, folk songs and the songs of the Polish partisans, as well as others from the Spanish civil war. It was the undisturbed den to which Grotowski and I retreated to drink cups of strong tea, a dark brew that was most effective in keeping us awake. We conjectured and discussed, listened to music, reread articles that I had

---

[14] Twenty years later, in 1983, I met Flaszen in Trappeto, near Palermo, at an international colloquium. Odin Teatret was presenting *Ashes of Brecht* and after the performance Flaszen approached me and confessed his surprise: 'In Poland I considered you an ingenuous Casanova. Yet you have put on a production which, together with Grotowski's *Akropolis* and Kantor's *The Dead Class*, is for me the most precise theatrical embodiment of cruelty and horror in history.'

written or else Grotowski dictated notes. We had long conversations which I then transcribed in the form of an interview entitled 'The New Testament of the Theatre'.

Here in this room we reread, word by word, the text of Wyspiański's *Akropolis* and Marlowe's *Doctor Faustus*, selecting and assembling the fragments to be used in the performance. We discussed articles in Polish magazines or reviews of the theatre's productions. Grotowski explained who had written them and with what aim in mind, as well as the possible repercussions on the local authorities who kept an anxious eye on his untraditional performances. Sometimes our dialogues were disconcertingly trite, with trivial anecdotes and coarse remarks, ironical comments and reciprocal gibes.

Almost every evening Grotowski and I went to the station restaurant which stayed open all night. It was our living room. We had supper and then, sipping continuous cups of tea - each with two tea bags - we talked for hours, often until dawn. Sometimes only one of us spoke in long monologues during which the other's presence served to make thoughts and memories, doubts and questions reverberate, giving them life and clothing them with words.

Grotowski talked of his fatherless childhood in a small provincial Polish town, of the books he had read, of Thomas Mann and Karl May, of his mother Emilia[15], of his political activity and his theatre studies in Cracow and Moscow, of his journey in Turkmenistan, of De Gaulle and Field Marshall Piłsudski. He was obsessed by Poland, but his patriotism was not nationalism. It was pride over the artists who would not be broken and subdued. He spent hours on end relating episodes from Polish history and literature. He was in love with the great Romantic writers Słowacki, Norwid and above all Mickiewicz. He knew long fragments by heart which he recited to me.

Litwo! Ojczyzno moja! ty jesteś jak zdrowie;
Ile cię trzeba cenić, ten tylko się dowie,
Kto cię stracił.

That was the beginning of *Pan Tadeusz* by Mickiewicz, and Grotowski

[15] Emilia Grotowski was a woman of great character who signified a lot for her son. She lived in Cracow and I made her acquaintance on Christmas Eve 1962 in a rather original way. Polish tradition dictates that an extra place be laid at table just in case, during the Christmas meal, the suffering Christ or any needy person should knock at the door. Grotowski and I had agreed that I should present myself at eight o'clock in the evening as a solitary stranger with no friends, while he and his mother were dining. His mother, who did not know me, invited me in and shared the food between the three of us. Only at the end of the meal did Grotowski tell her who I was.

let himself be lulled by the melodic softness of the lines: 'O Lithuania, my fatherland, you are like health. Only one who has lost you can truly appreciate you.' Lithuania, where Mickiewicz was born, had belonged to Poland at the time of the great Polish monarchs. Grotowski described to me the insurrections against the Russians, the exile of the intellectuals and the peregrinations of Mickiewicz. There was always a clear anti-Soviet subtext (but this was common in the Poland of those times. The Russians had huge military bases, one of which was not far from Opole.) He often quoted a fragment of the third part of *Dziady*, enjoying the nastiness with which Mickiewicz narrates the episode of a Russian soldier who is flogged for fainting after a long parade under the sun:

Ach, żal mi ciebie, biedny Słowianinie!
Biedny narodzie! Żal mi twojej doli,
Jeden znasz tylko heroizm – niewoli.

'I pity you, poor Slav! O wretched nation! I lament your destiny. You know only one heroism: the heroism of slavery.' He often dwelt on Field Marshall Piłsudski who had defeated the Red Army in 1920 and allowed Poland to regain its independence.

I told him of my fatherless childhood in a small town in the south of Italy and of the books I had read, of Salgari and Knut Hamsun, of my mother Vera and the military school in Naples, of Atatürk and Ibn Saud, solitary builders of nations, of my political activity in Oslo, of the thousand ways to survive among foreigners and of my wanderings, of my experiences as a worker and of the ports I had visited as a sailor.

All this we told each other with a quiet zeal, like two Sheherezades whose tortuous eloquence was embellished by contrasts and paradoxes, polishing phrases, searching for ambiguous or hermaphrodite expressions, dilating the rhythm, whispering, without fear of pauses. We sat at that dilapidated table, fighting against the night, amid the rank smell of beer and cigarette smoke, the drowsy atmosphere and the grime, interrupted by the din of the loudspeaker announcing the arrivals and departures of trains. Then our narrations-confessions would resume and, as ineluctably as a river flowing into the sea, would end up in that India 'which exists before the eyes of our soul'. Hinduism was our privileged point of encounter. Ramana Maharishi (not to be confused with the guru of transcendental meditation) had played an important part in the life of Grotowski, and Ramakrishna in mine.

We spoke of the techniques of the various *darsana* (the different points of view of Hinduism) of Shankara and his Advaita Vedanta, of the *bhakti* (the religious fervour of Ramanuja) of Patanjali and his texts on hatha yoga, of Mahayana Buddhism and its Ch'an and Zen currents, of Nagarjuna and his Madhyamika or New School of Wisdom which preaches the doctrine of *Sunyata*. *Sunyata*, the Void, is not nothingness. It is non-duality in which the object does not differ from the subject. The self and belief in the self are the causes of error and pain. The way to escape from error and pain is to eliminate the self. This is the Perfect Wisdom, the enlightenment that can be attained through a *via negativa*, denying worldly categories and phenomenons to the point of denying the self and, by so doing, reaching the Void.

Sunyata is the conjunction between yes and no, existence and non-existence. It is the moment in which recognition and rejection, assertion and refusal blend. In the Buddhist tradition *Sunyata* is the absolute negation of this world by means of a technique based not on rational thought but on experience. It is a practice which stands midway between affirmation and negation, between action and the renunciation of action. As long as one wants to achieve enlightenment, it remains unobtainable because when one desires something, there is a duality: a self which aims towards the desired end, and a non-self towards which one aims. True attainment is reached only when one no longer wishes to attain something. In *Towards a Poor Theatre* Grotowski applied this vision to the actor: 'The requisite state of mind is a passive readiness to realise an active role, a state in which one does not *want to do something* but rather *cannot help not doing it*'[16].

Grotowski was well acquainted with the philosophy of *Sunyata*. In 1957 and 1958 he had given a series of lectures in Cracow on 'Eastern philosophical thought' in which he had spoken often of Nagarjuna. In March 1960, a year after he had taken over the direction of the Teatr 13 Rzędów, he did a production for Cracow radio of *Nagarjuna*, based on his own scenario. In this vision of *Sunyata* it is possible to glimpse the source of the first definition that Grotowski gave his method: 'a dialectic of affirming and surpassing', which he later changed to 'dialectic of apotheosis and derision'. One can also see how *Sunyata* inspired his *via negativa* to describe the essence of theatre: the relationship between actor and spectator.

We dwelt at length on Sariputra and Buddhism's Old School of Wisdom which, as a means of defeating the enemy – the passions – concentrated on the psychic powers of the individual and founded schools of occult powers within the sects of Tantric Buddhism and

---

[16] Ibidem, page 17. The italics are Grotowski's.

Lamaism. Then our conversation slid from Tantrism of the Left Hand to Milarepa and Marpa, his severe master; to Angelus Silesius and Chuang-tsu, to the Tao te king and the Upanishads, to the Gospels and their protagonist as described by Ernest Renan in his *Life of Jesus*: a nihilist who always turned the other cheek, a solitary *provocateur* who knew about the precariousness of existence: the Son of Man has nowhere to lay his head.

On occasions we would pause over Gurdjieff and Ouspensky, their books and their techniques (the 'stop' in Gurdjieff's dances had been incorporated in the training exercises). Grotowski had a great admiration for the way in which Gurdjieff had succeeded in creating an 'Institute for the Harmonious Development of Mankind' in Tiflis while the Soviets were in power and using this anodyne name to hide the practices which were going on within it. Also the way that Gurdjieff had managed to bring all his collaborators to safety was a lesson in how to protect the essential in adverse political circumstances: they all went for long walks in the mountains, as though this were a part of the programme of 'Harmonious Development'. In this way the Soviet soldiers became accustomed to seeing them walking alone or in small groups through the mountains bordering on Turkey. One fine day all the members of the Institute, with Gurdjieff at their head, crossed into Turkey and remained there.

We moved on to alchemy, shamanism, trance, rituals, the *misterium tremendum et fascinans*, and at this point the same nucleus of writers reappeared: Jung, Durkheim, Lévy-Bruhl, Mauss, Lévi-Strauss, Caillois, Bachelard and Eliade. Their texts made us reflect out loud, and we used ourselves and our own experiences to investigate the fertile zone of 'archetypes', of 'collective representations', of 'wild thought'. We commented on them, paraphrased them; they inspired in us endless suppositions and hypotheses. These were the sources we tapped in an unceasing reformulation of a vision of theatre.

For me it was important to find terms that were both appropriate and suggestive to epitomise the features of this new theatre. In my writings I yielded to invention: theatre as an anthropological expedition, performance as psychomachia, as a clash between, on the one hand, the psychic process of the actors as they lay themselves bare and, on the other, the spectators who want to defend their certainties and psychic wellbeing. I used the expression 'self-penetration' to characterise the actor's inner process in this theatre which was not yet defined as 'poor'. It was not a question of terminology but of faith. I firmly believed that Grotowski's way of thinking would shake the ancient edifice of theories and routines, that his words were the Word, the New Testament of the Theatre. I wanted to witness, to spread the Word, to act as a proselyte. And then we ordered another cup of strong tea, thanking Bodhidharma for the umpteenth time that he had caused the birth of the plant in China. Once, after he had fallen asleep during meditation, he had cut off his eyelids, and where they fell to the ground the tea plant with its benevolent leaves had grown up to help combat drowsiness.

Sometimes we were interrupted by Jerzy Falkowski, a brilliant journalist who was always in a hurry. He had come from Warsaw to interview Grotowski and, fascinated by his theatre as well as by a pretty girl, he had remained in Opole. He introduced himself into our conversation by telling us the latest news and the gossip from artistic-political circles, both local and national. Once he appeared at three o'clock in the morning, flitting about like a joyful swallow. An hour previously he had telephoned a local writer: 'I am Jerzy Andrzejewski (one of the greatest Polish writers) and I have just arrived in Opole. I have read your books and I appreciate them enormously. I was thinking of coming to visit you at home...' 'Please be my guest and do come over straight away', replied the writer who had been asleep in bed but was proud to receive such a prestigious call. Then Falkowski had rung another local writer, repeating the same story: 'I am Jerzy Andrzejewski and I have just arrived in Opole. I have read your books etc., etc. ...' And he received another invitation. After this he had called back to the first writer: 'Listen, I have just met a colleague of ours (local writer No. 2) and when I told him I was on my way over to see you he was flabbergasted. Apparently you never stop criticising me and my books...' Writer No. 1 had protested that this was slander and that he had a boundless admiration for Andrzejewski's works. 'Right, then I shall come to your house', replied Falkowski-Andrzejewski who had immediately called writer No. 2 again and repeated the same story. For an hour Falkowski had alternated telephone calls, taking his revenge on two rather disagreeable intellectuals.

I can still recall the dismal restaurant; its floor covered with cigarette ends, the stale smell of cabbage from the *bigos* soup, the thick smoky atmosphere, the few drowsy half-drunk customers and Grotowski and me laughing fit to burst at Falkowski's perfidious imagination and sense of justice[17]. This scene comes to mind every time that the 'guru' Grotowski and his lack of humour is mentioned. As does yet another memory. We were hitchhiking back to Opole from a nearby town where my leaflet on

[17] Falkowski died suddenly a few years later, while rushing to the broadcasting studio. The autopsy showed that his heart had literally split in two. When Grotowski told me about it in Holstebro, our comment was unanimous: how lucky he was to die running.

the Teatr 13 Rzędów was being printed. We walked along the road boldly raising our arms to every passing car. A ZIM, the Russian-made car used by the *nomenklatura*, stopped and the Secretary of Opole's Communist Party stuck his head out of the window. Grotowski and I immediately reverted to serious and responsible expressions: unfortunately we had missed our train. There was only room in the ZIM for Grotowski, so I continued on alone, reflecting on the astonished face of the Secretary, on Grotowski's expressive capacity and on the wisdom of Karen Blixen: 'I shall know you, not by your face, but by your mask'.

Pulsation, Rhythm, Movement

We spoke too about theatre. There was one very precise domain of experiences, texts and biographies that we returned to again and again. It consisted of Stanislavsky (a great deal), Meyerhold (much less), Vachtangov (whom I suspected was the director whose productions appealed most to Grotowski), Dullin (his text on improvisation was much appreciated) and Delsarte (whose principles of introversion and extroversion had been introduced into the training). Another point of reference was Marcel Marceau's mime. Grotowski had seen him in France in 1959 and had published an enthusiastic article about him. Some mime exercises had been incorporated in the training[18].

Countless references were made to Polish artists such as Witkacy, Iwo Gall and the Reduta laboratory whose two founders, Juliusz Osterwa and Mieczysław Limanowski, Grotowski good-humouredly chided for dressing their actors in uniforms and insisting on a sober life while they escaped at night from their theatre-monastery to enjoy themselves. But the irony was based on admiration. He told me several times about the helpfulness and discipline of Halina Gallowa, a previous actress of Reduta whom Grotowski had directed in *The Chairs* by Ionesco, his first production in 1957 at the Teatr Poezji in Cracow. He was also very attached to Irena and Tadeusz Byrski who had written a letter of support when, in 1960, the critics had torn to pieces his two first productions – Cocteau's *Orpheus* and Byron's *Cain* – while on tour in Warsaw[19].

[18] When Marceau was in Wrocław in 1963 to visit one of Henrik Tomaszewski's actresses, I went to try to convince him to come to Opole. Unfortunately Marceau could not be tempted to meet someone he did not know. It was for this fascination with mime that Jacques Lecoq reproached Grotowski. Each time I met Lecoq he could not resist telling me how surprised he was to see something as trite as the scene where the actors 'walked against the wind' in *The Constant Prince*.
[19] Many critics laid special emphasis on the low, almost amateurish technical level of the actors, cf. Zbigniew Osiński, *Grotowski i jego Laboratorium*, Państwowy Instytut Wydawniczy,

For the first year and a half we rarely spoke of Asian theatre. I had seen a few performances in Singapore, Hong Kong, Shanghai and Calcutta when I was a sailor. I remembered almost nothing; they had left no traces in my memory. Grotowski had been to China in August 1962 for three weeks and had come back with many impressions and a great deal of information. He had noticed that in the Peking Opera the actors begin an action by starting out in the opposite direction to where they want to end up. If they want to move to the left, they take a step towards the right and then go to their objective on the left. This observation became an effective working tool that we baptised 'the Chinese principle', and under the same name it also entered into the terminology and the practice of Odin Teatret. Grotowski had also been struck by a meeting he had had in Shanghai with a Dr. Ling, a voice specialist. Dr. Ling had shown him how to check whether the larynx was open or closed when an actor was speaking. This form of control was incorporated into the vocal training, and was meticulously described by me on page 142 of *In Search of Lost Theatre*.

The situation changed somewhat after my trip to India from July to December 1963. I had travelled there by car, crossing Europe, Turkey, Iran and Pakistan. Amongst the various forms of Indian theatre that I saw, Kathakali from Kerala had made the greatest impression on me. I studied it for three weeks, noting down the physical exercises, those for developing the mobility of the eyes and of the facial muscles, and the gaits. I reported on all this on my return to Opole and for a short period some of the exercises were added to the training.

Grotowski and I often referred to Asian theatre, but most of our knowledge came from articles or books. The constellation from which we used to take our bearings was made up of archetypes, rituals, trance, shamanism, certain schools of Hindu and Buddhist philosophy and the

Warsaw 1980. Zbigniew Osiński who is at present a Professor at Warsaw University, has the great merit of having preserved the memory of events from the life and work of Grotowski in this book with its wealth of significant minutiae and essential details. Unfortunately only one translation exists in America, completely disfigured by cuts and reduced to a digest of chronological notes. Osiński, a young university assistant, arrived in Opole one day in 1963 from Poznań after seeing *Akropolis*. He stayed a few days, following the work at the Teatr 13 Rzędów and returning whenever he had a little spare time. From then on he has followed Grotowski's path in Poland and abroad. After the dissolution of the Teatr-Laboratorium and Grotowski's definitive move first to the USA and then to Italy, Osiński defended the historical premises in Wrocław and, with courage and considerable sacrifice, created the Ośrodek Badań Twórczości Jerzego Grotowskiego i Poszukiwań Teatralno-Kulturowych (Centre of Studies on Jerzy Grotowski's Work and of Cultural and Theatrical Research) which is not only a fundamental archive for this theatre, but also promotes international performances, meetings and seminars of high quality.

tradition of the *Wielka Reforma*, the Great Reform, that is the experiences of the innovators of European theatre during the first thirty years of the twentieth century.

Grotowski was not very familiar with the different forms of classical Asian theatre. It was certain aspects of Indian philosophy that were crucial to his vision of the world, permeating his existential attitude and his theatre practice. This was traceable in the smallest detail of the dramaturgy or technical composition. I spoke at length to Grotowski about this conviction of mine in Pontedera in 1992, teasing him about the imaginatively elaborate relationships with Asian theatre that critics and scholars had attributed to him. In my view he was only interested in one thing: India or rather Hinduism. Grotowski confirmed this, and told me that he owed his 'secret vocation' for India to his mother, Emilia, who was a 'Hinduist'. He also spoke to me yet again of the importance of Paul Brunton's book, *A Search in Secret India*, that his mother had made him read at the age of eight or nine when they were refugees in the village of Nienadówka during the Second World War. The chapters on the life of Ramana Maharishi had made a particular impression on him. In December 1976 Grotowski had made his fourth and last journey to India with his mother and together they had visited Arunachala, the mountain to which Maharishi had retreated.

This influence from Hinduism was present in Grotowski from his very first steps in theatre. In 1960, when he was twenty-seven, a year after he became director of the Teatr 13 Rzędów, he wrote:

If I had to define our scenic research in a single term I would refer to the myth of the Dance of Shiva. (...) It is an attempt to absorb reality in all its aspects, with its multiplicity of facets yet at the same time remaining outside and distant. To express it another way, it is the dance of form, the pulsation of form, the flowing and fissile multiplicity of theatre conventions, styles, acting traditions. But it is also the construction of contraries: the intellectual game in impetuosity, the seriousness in the grotesque, the mockery in pain. It is the dance that shatters every theatrical illusion, every 'verisimilitude with life' and at the same time nourishes the ambition (never satiated, of course) to retreat into oneself, absorbing and embracing human destiny in its totality.(...)

Ancient Indian theatre, like ancient Japanese and Greek theatre, was a ritual which identified itself with dance, mime and acting. The performance was not a 'representation of reality' (the construction of an illusion), but a 'dance' of reality (an artificial construction, similar to a 'rhythmic vision' that recalls reality. (...)

There is a mythological quotation in which Shiva says: I am without name, without form, without action. I am pulsation, movement and rhythm (Shiva-gita). *The essence of the theatre for which we are searching is 'pulsation, movement and rhythm'* [20].

The dance of Shiva of which Grotowski speaks is not a metaphor. It is a personal vision of existence which, on the actor's technical level is translated as organicity (pulsation and rhythm), on a dramaturgical level as the simultaneous presence of opposites (dialectic of apotheosis and derision) and on an aesthetic level as performance which refuses to give the illusion of reality and attempts to recreate the contractions, the dilations and the contrasts: its 'dance'.

Between ourselves, Grotowski and I spoke of two types of techniques and we defined them as 'technique 1' and 'technique 2'[21]. 'Technique 1' referred to the vocal and physical possibilities and to the various methods of psycho-technique handed down to us since Stanislavsky. This 'technique 1', which could be complex and sophisticated, could be achieved through *rzemiosło*, i.e. the theatre craft.

'Technique 2' aimed at releasing the 'spiritual' energy in each of us. It was a practical path which concentrated the self on the self and, by overcoming subjectivity, opened the way to the regions known to shamans, yogi and mystics where all the individual psychic forces are integrated. We believed profoundly in the capacity of the actor to gain access to this 'technique 2'. We imagined its path and we searched for the precise steps which might help to penetrate into the dark night of one's inner energy.

If today I were to define Grotowski's attitude throughout his entire active life, whether in theatre or on its periphery, I would adopt the Sanskrit term *sâdhanâ* which is untranslatable into any European language and means simultaneously: spiritual quest, method and practice.

We never spoke of Artaud. I did not know of him and nor perhaps did Grotowski. I first heard him mentioned by Raymonde Temkine when she came to Opole at Easter 1963. This is all the more amusing since, from 1958 to 1959, I had studied French literature at Oslo University, specialising in the twentieth century. However, Artaud was not held in any regard either as a poet or a writer, and his myth emerged only when Gallimard, between 1961 and 1964, published the first three volumes of his *Complete*

---

[20] Zbigniew Osiński, *Grotowski wytycza trasy*, Wydawnictwo Pusty Obłok, Warsaw 1993, pp. 122-123. This is a statement by Grotowski at the Circle of Friends of the Teatr 13 Rzędów in September 1960 during rehearsals of *Shakuntala*. Grotowski presented this text when he did his exam in direction that same October at the Cracow theatre school.
[21] See also letter 13 from Grotowski of 6 February 1965.

Works with his manifestos and texts on theatre.

While drinking tea and smoking *Extra Mocne* – cigarettes similar to Gauloises – Grotowski and I discussed the day's rehearsals, the various problems experienced by the actors and the possible ways of overcoming them. Grotowski explained to me in detail the reasons for his decisions, and for any changes and interventions. He pointed out why he behaved in a particular way with one actor but did not use the same approach with another. He was very aware of the psychological make-up of each individual and directed them accordingly. It was not a question of working on their psychology in relation to a character but rather how, *involuntarily*, to draw out certain characteristics and personal energies in order to colour the scenic action.

It was in an attempt to resolve such a problem that the training came into being. During the first rehearsals for *Akropolis* (March-April 1962), Ewa Lubowiecka (an actress who left the performance before it was finished) continually slid into emotive tones. The action took place in Auschwitz and on no account did Grotowski want any sentimentality. He then had the idea of freezing the faces of the actors as if they were of stone, and therefore also the exceedingly expressive face of Ewa Lubowiecka, thereby creating 'masks' without the help of make-up, but relying entirely on the effectiveness of the facial muscles. During the whole performance the face had to remain immobilised in a single expression that evoked that of the 'muslims', as the prisoners in Auschwitz were called when they reached the last stage of survival.

The search began for this 'mask' which, according to Grotowski, would fix a reaction typical of the personality of each actor. By means of a series of devices and without ever revealing his aim, Grotowski guided each single actor in a different way to produce scowls and sneers, servile and submissive airs, countenances that were timorous and defiant. They had an organic force, an amazing emotive impact and, in spite of being artificial, they had nothing of the grimace.

A particular time was established, during rehearsals, for creating the 'masks'. Then it was extended to allow the actors to practise the gaits and positions of imbalance which were to characterise the behaviour of the prisoners. New elements began to be included that were only indirectly connected with the performance: acrobatics, composition, respiratory and vocal exercises. This particular time, which was separate from the rehearsals, was called *ćwiczenia* (exercises). The amazing thing – which had profound historical consequences – was that these continued even when the rehearsals ended, acquiring an autonomy of their own.

Already while preparing *Shakuntala* the actors had been doing exercises connected with the tasks that arose out of the working process. The same had occurred with *Kordian*. But these exercises had always been pragmatic, serving the performance's objectives, and were abandoned once rehearsals were ended. Only after *Akropolis* did the actors continue with the exercises which acquired a value of their own, and were no longer subjected to the demands of a specific performance.

Every day the actors met at the theatre to train. The exercises which were directly linked to *Akropolis* were eliminated, others were modified and new ones were added. Grotowski entrusted each of the actors with the responsibility for a specific field, becoming the inspiration and advisor for each of them. Zygmunt Molik was responsible for the vocal exercises (the famous resonators), Rena Mirecka for the plastic exercises and composition, Zbigniew Cynkutis for the rhythmics (which he had learnt at the Łódź theatre school) and Ryszard Cieślak for acrobatics. During that period I was particularly impressed by the technical qualities of Rena Mirecka and Zygmunt Molik.

Through practice and modification the exercises changed character and name. In 1964 the different sectors, with their respective instructors, were defined as follows in *In Search of Lost Theatre* (page 117): Physical and rhythmic exercises - R. Cieślak; plastic and eye exercises - A. Jahołkowski; vocal and respiratory exercises - Z. Molik; facial exercises - R. Mirecka[22].

From the very beginning the term *ćwiczenie*, exercise, became important for Grotowski and Flaszen. It was the perfect word which concealed meaningful allusions behind a neutral and concise facade. The term was used publicly for the first time in April 1963 in the programme for *Doctor Faustus*, the production which followed *Akropolis*. There is a section in the programme entitled 'Theatrical exercises' which does not give an explanation of the training, its method or objective, but quotes fragments of

---

[22] In 1968 in *Towards A Poor Theatre* (p.133) Grotowski makes these comments on my description of the exercises from 1964: 'During this time, I was searching for a positive technique or, in other words, a certain method of training capable of objectively giving the actor a creative skill that was rooted in his imagination and his personal associations. Certain elements from these exercises were retained in the training during the period that followed, but their aim has changed. All the exercises which merely constituted an answer to the question: "How can this be done?" were eliminated. The exercises have now become a pretext for working out a personal form of training. The actor must discover those resistances and obstacles which hinder him in his creative task. Thus the exercises become a means of overcoming these personal impediments. The actor no longer asks himself: "How can I do this?". Instead, he must know what not to do, what obstructs him. (...) This is what I mean by *via negativa*: a process of elimination.'

Polish and foreign articles on the theatre in Opole. It is introduced by a rather revealing but unsigned note which is almost certainly by Flaszen:

We are publishing here fragments of articles on the working method and the productions of the Teatr-Laboratorium 13 Rzędów. They are gathered under the title THEATRICAL EXERCISES since this is the term we like to use, in our own internal jargon, to define the working technique of the 13 Rzędów. Doubtless the term THEATRICAL EXERCISES is not a particularly impressive one, but it has its positive sides. It emphasises the concrete character which distinguishes our method. It helps us to underline the fact that for us this method is similar to a road or a springboard, and has absolutely no doctrinal value; that the system of work cannot be separated here from the actor's training; that for us every role, every production, should not be an objective in itself but rather an exercise, the preparation for an even more complex exercise, the penetration into hitherto unexplored regions. What is more, the term THEATRICAL EXERCISES also permits a parallel that we find amusing – an allusion to the 'operationes spirituales'; but that is already anecdote.

Intelligentibus pauca. Alluding to 'spiritual operations', Flaszen refers to Ignatius Loyola's active meditation and 'spiritual exercises', a practice which Eisenstein had already mentioned with regard to Stanislavsky's system. Flaszen barely touches on the subject in order to avoid interference by the communist censors towards such an 'idealistic' and 'mystical' attitude. But he clearly indicates the complementary potentialities of the training: the actor's craftsman-like work on him- or herself, and at the same time an *operatio spiritualis*. This conception is to be found at the very heart of Grotowski's various activities after 1970, when he abandoned theatre production as well as research strictly connected to the actor and the spectator.

Censors and Allies

Throughout those years, censorship controlled every form of expression in Poland: performances, public meetings and every type of publication even if it was only a visiting card. A theatre received clearance permission for the text it wanted to present and then, shortly before the premiere, the performance was checked to make sure it contained nothing that might displease the regime. The motives for censorship could vary according to the circumstances: formalistic or decadent tendencies, virulent anti-religious feelings (at a time when the Party wanted to be on good terms with the Catholic church), anti-Soviet allusions, idealism and cosmopolitanism. I mention the formalistic and anti-religious aspects because those were amongst the arguments used by the Opole authorities to criticise

Grotowski. His Faustus, rebelling against God, neither won the sympathies of the clerics nor even of the Marxists since he wanted to be a saint and spoke a religious language, saturated with mystical allusions. What is more, the actors' technique, explicit in its theatricality, was the object of disapprobation even though it was tolerated in other theatres.

But dictatorships, especially those which are bland and not unnecessarily cruel, as was the case with Poland at the beginning of the sixties, also show a human side: solidarity and corruption. One of the Opole censors was sincerely attached to Grotowski and came to performances also in an unofficial capacity. One evening in my room, where I had invited him for a cup of tea together with Grotowski, he began to sing a religious hymn:

Ludu, mój ludu,

cóżem ci uczynił?

W czymem zasmucił albo w czym zawinił?

Jam cię wyzwolił z mocy Faraona,

a tyś przyrzadził krzyż na me ramiona.

'O my people/ what have I done to you?/ I freed you from the power of the Pharaoh/ and you placed a cross on my shoulders.'

Grotowski also began to sing religious hymns, and then they moved on to the kolendy or Christmas songs. I listened for some time to those melodies which were so deeply rooted in Poland and which Grotowski had used with such refined cruelty in Akropolis. During rehearsals for Doctor Faustus a few days later, while searching together with Zbigniew Cynkutis for the blasphemous formula which Faustus would use to conjure up Mephistopheles, Grotowski proposed the hymn of the censor. Faustus invokes Evil with the heart-rending and mournful lament of Christ, demonstrating the wickedness of the Father who sacrifices His Son.

That same censor helped me with the publication of a booklet (Expériences du théâtre laboratoire 13 Rzędów) in April 1962. He found a printer, spoke with the director and everything went smoothly thanks to the donation of a considerable sum to 'facilitate' contacts, in addition to covering the printing costs. This human feature of the regime (which people call corruption) was also important later on when I published another booklet, and again when I 'borrowed' a bus from a jam factory.

Once a month I went to Warsaw to collect my scholarship. I visited friends and acquaintances: fellow students from the university and the theatre school, foreign students, intellectuals, artists, theatre people and those I had involved in the issue of Sipario on Polish theatre. Nobody could understand what on earth I was doing in a hole like Opole. Hardly

59

anyone had heard of Grotowski, and the few who had seen his first two productions during the disastrous Warsaw tour in 1960, could not understand what I found so extraordinary about that small provincial theatre. I spent hours on end describing Grotowski's theories and productions amidst the irony and bewilderment of whoever listened to me. I felt like Kordian, brimming over with enthusiasm and good intentions, yet considered insane by others.

But all of this bore fruit. I met Zenobiusz Strzelecki, a renowned scenographer, who was just finishing a monumental history of Polish scenography. I had asked him for an article for *Sipario*, but had told him so much about Gurawski and Grotowski, giving him drawings and other material, that in the end he inserted an appendix in his book which had already gone to press. Both he and his wife, the critic Krystyna Mazur, became friends and often invited me to their home when I was in Warsaw.

None of my acquaintances escaped my agitprop zeal and missionary activism for the Theatre's New Testament. And I would make a point of tracking down those I didn't know to talk of the Teatr 13 Rzędów: the poet Zbigniew Herbert, the humorist Stanisław Jerzy Lec, the theatre historian Zbigniew Raszewski and the critics Edward Csató, Andrzej Drawicz, Jerzy Koenig, Wojciech Natanson and Jerzy Pomianowski. This happened in the first half of 1962 when Grotowski had finished *Kordian*, *Akropolis* was still in the making and there were no serious problems with the authorities.

It was mainly my foreign friends who listened to me. Some of them became extremely effective allies. Mike Elster, a Briton who was studying film directing in Łódź came to see me in Opole and in 1963 he decided to make the film for his final exam on Grotowski's theatre. *Letter from Opole* is the oldest documentary of some substance on the Teatr-Laboratorium 13 Rzędów, with scenes from the daily life of the actors, from the training and from *Doctor Faustus*. It is of considerable historical interest because it shows both the structure of the small 'traditional' theatre and the training, then only in its early stages. It is therefore an unavoidable testimony for anyone who wishes to compare the successive development of the exercises documented in Torgeir Wethal's film on Ryszard Cieślak's training from 1972[23].

---

[23] Mike Elster had a friend, Michael Kustow, with whom he had studied at Oxford. He was a young critic working with the Royal Shakespeare Company as well as being the editor of an influential magazine, *Encore*, which had contributors such as Peter Brook and Charles Marowitz. Elster brought Kustow to Opole and in September 1963 the latter published a long and evocative article entitled *Ludens mysterium tremendum et fascinosum*. When Grotowski came to England for the first time in 1965, for my wedding, it was through Mike Elster and his friends that he met Peter Brook.

Also my close friend, Erik Veaux, who corrected the articles I wrote in French, came to Opole and became Grotowski's translator. He began to write about him in France and was a valuable and ever-willing guide during Grotowski's first visits to Paris when he was still unknown.

How to Be Both Dove and Snake

Thanks to my Italian passport I could travel in and out of Poland at will. I took advantage of this to make a few brief trips abroad. These had the dual objective of spreading the Theatre's New Testament while giving the critics and the hostile Polish authorities the impression that Grotowski was known abroad. In my room or in the station restaurant Grotowski and I planned my itinerary. The intention was to place my articles on the Teatr 13 Rzędów with magazines and newspapers, to contact political parties, theatre personalities and artistic circles, telling them about the theatre in Opole and leaving articles, photos, drawings and other material with them. That was how I began to write. I used French because it was an international language and more widely understood than my own, Italian. Furthermore, Paris was still *the* cultural centre for Poles and for many other nations.

These trips abroad helped me to overcome any timidity about speaking in public or in approaching famous people, and forced me to find the incisiveness necessary to convince people. Within me, vivid scenes, details, facial expressions and voices from *Akropolis* or *Doctor Faustus* gave me strength and boosted my courage. I identified emotionally and intellectually with the universe of Grotowski's ideas and activity, *our* theatre. Every other form of theatre seemed to me, to paraphrase Nagarjuna, to be 'the son of a sterile virgin sculpted in stone', very beautiful maybe, but with no soul. The desire to protect the work of Grotowski, of whom I was very fond, and that tiny theatre which for me was home, adventure, passion and religion, became a permanent challenge, an obsession, a necessity. My task to defend all of this comprised fighting, astuteness, subterfuge and the capacity to make decisions and act rapidly. It meant being both a dove and a snake, every day and every moment. I discovered within me faculties that had until then been dormant. Kabir knew of this and had written about it in a poem:

The perfect Master is the true hero
who shoots the Word like a single arrow.
Struck, you fall to earth
and a wound opens up in the depth of your soul.

All my worldly wealth consisted of 2400 zlotys from my scholarship, which corresponded to the salary of a high school teacher. This could not be changed into foreign currency and not even train tickets to travel abroad could be paid for with Polish money. Sometimes I was lucky and succeeded in exchanging a few zlotys for dollars with some foreign student who had just arrived. My only source of earnings was the occasional payment for an article, mainly from Scandinavian newspapers and magazines. Every cent had to bear fruit as though it were a million. My meagre savings in dollars were only used for essentials: train tickets. The generosity of friends and casual acquaintances was my capital.

It was my custom to travel by night so that I could sleep in the train. Problems arose if I stayed several days in a town. I spent nights at friends' houses, if I had any, or else slept in public parks, doorways or in buildings under construction. However, the following morning I had to be clean and well dressed in order to make a good impression on the people I met. The station, where I left my few belongings at the left luggage office, was my beauty salon. The most difficult things were shaving with a razor and shaving cream, and washing my shirts which smelt of perspiration since I slept in my clothes. I entered the labyrinth of each new town with, as an Ariadne's thread, a list of names and addresses which I had acquired or been given. Under my arm I clutched the bag containing photos of Grotowski's productions, my booklets in French or else my latest articles, and Gurawski's drawings (photocopies didn't exist and it took hours and hours to prepare several copies).

My first stop was always Vienna where I installed myself at the home of the Polish playwright, Artur Maria Swinarski. He was an elderly and sardonic homosexual whom I had met when I first arrived in Warsaw, and who had been allowed to leave Poland. He treated me magnificently, while reproaching me for not wanting to pay homage on the same side of Eros's alter as himself. He made me eat delicacies which were not to be found in Poland, covered me with small presents and constantly teased me about my 'craze' for that rogue Grotowski who was capable only of destroying beautiful plays. He introduced me to his friends in artistic and journalistic circles. It was at his house that I met the young Austrian playwright Adolf Opel who, without knowing it, made an important contribution to Grotowski and his theatre.

It was my custom to ask everybody I met if they knew of anyone who might be interested in the experiences of the theatre in Opole. Opel gave me a few names amongst which was that of Renée Saurel who was the theatre critic for *Les Temps Modernes*, Jean Paul Sartre's magazine in Paris, and also James Hatch, an American professor teaching at Cairo University in Egypt. A few days later, on my arrival in Paris, I rang Renée Saurel and she invited me to her home. She was a courageous woman, a nonconformist, and was immediately interested in what I had to tell. I gave her a type-written copy in French of my book *In Search of Lost Theatre* and she did her utmost to find a publisher for it. She was not successful, but when the book was published in Italy in 1965 she wrote a nine-page review of it in *Les Temps Modernes* which had international repercussions, and also created echoes throughout Poland where Sartre's magazine enjoyed great prestige. Renée Saurel wrote often and competently about Grotowski, well before she got to know him in person. Then when Grotowski came to France they became friends and she followed his activities with a loyal and objective passion.

I made a parcel of various materials including photos, my booklets in French and Gurawski's drawings, and sent them to James Hatch in Cairo, the other name given to me by Adolf Opel. He replied to me in Opole expressing his interest and asking me to send some material to a friend of his at the University of New Orleans. His friend's name was Richard Schechner. At that time I was accustomed to contacting people like Mircea Eliade or Fernando Arrabal. So why not this Richard Schechner?

I heard from Schechner in the spring of 1963. His letter was a big surprise: he was editor of the magazine *Tulane Drama Review* and was preparing an issue on Marlowe. He asked for more information and photos of *Doctor Faustus*, on which Grotowski had been working. I immediately sent him a description of the production and of the way in which Grotowski had assembled and interpreted the text. In the summer of 1964 the *Tulane Drama Review* reported for the first time in America on the Teatr-Laboratorium 13 Rzędów. By mistake, Schechner printed my article under the name of Grotowski, a misunderstanding that amused us greatly: Grotowski boasted to me about his talent as a writer, and I accused him of graphomania. In the spring of 1965 the *Tulane Drama Review* published the translation of my two French booklets: *Expériences du théâtre-laboratoire 13 Rzędów* and *Le théâtre comme auto-pénétration collective* which also included Flaszen's important article on *Akropolis* as well as a series of excerpts from European articles on Grotowski.

In 1967 Schechner, who was a searching intellectual and an audacious theatre director, participated in a seminar held by Grotowski in Montreal, Canada. In December of the same year he helped in inviting Grotowski to New York University where he taught. Together with Jacques Chwat, Theodore Hoffman and Mary Tierney, he made a long collective interview with Grotowski which was published in the *TDR-Tulane Drama Review* in autumn 1968. With his Performance Group, Schechner drew inspiration from Grotowski's theories and training, theorising an *environmental theatre* which achieved a wide diffusion. Throughout all these years Schechner has maintained a lively interest in Grotowski and his activities, and has often devoted ample space to them in the *TDR*[24].

After the stop in Vienna, my journey could follow three routes: down into Italy, back up to Paris and from there return to Poland; or, by way of Switzerland, aim straight for Paris; or else go north to Denmark, Sweden and Norway where it was easier to sell my articles to the newspapers and, above all, where they paid me immediately.

In Rome I stayed with my mother who fed her 'artist' son on her pension. There I visited the painter Achille Perilli who had organised some happenings, and sent me to see Alfredo Giuliani, a poet from Group 63. At the University I met Angelo Maria Ripellino. Discussion with him was a pleasure; he was so knowledgeable about the Slavonic world and instantaneously grasped and enjoyed the faintest allusion. To my astonishment, I discovered that there was a theatre laboratory led by an actor-director called Carmelo Bene. Delighted to find a 'kinsman' in Italy, I was preparing to get in touch with him when I read that he had urinated on a spectator (or a critic?) from the stage. Imagining how the Polish authorities would have reacted to this typical gesture of an artist from a decadent capitalist society, I deemed it wise not to associate his name with that of Grotowski[25]. I sneaked into the presentation ceremony for a book on Polish theatre and lamented to the author, Lamberto Trezzini, that he had not mentioned Grotowski. I contacted the left-wing newspapers *Paese Sera*, *L'Unità* and *Rinascita*, and the young communist weekly *Nuova Generazione* published an article of mine in March 1964 under the pseudonym Gösta Marcus[26].

I sent material to the composer Luigi Nono, who was interested in avant-garde theatre, and to Ferruccio Masini, a professor in Florence who subsequently wrote on Grotowski in *La Regione* in January 1963. In June 1963 I finally met Franco Quadri in person, the editor of *Sipario* with whom I had had a continual correspondence over the issue on

---

[24] In 1997 Richard Schechner and Lisa Wolford edited *The Grotowski Sourcebook* (Routledge, London and New York), a volume of 514 pages which gathers contributions from different parts of the world and illustrates the various phases in Grotowski's development.

[25] In fact, Carmelo Bene never urinated on a spectator, but the legend which was spread and repeated by the most philistine of newspapers on the basis of a tempestuous theatrical evening in Rome, followed him for a long time.

[26] I sometimes wrote under a pseudonym to give the impression that many people were interested in the Teatr 13 Rzędów.

Polish theatre[27].

In Switzerland I visited the Jung Institute in Zurich, leaving behind a pile of material for its director, James Hillman. In Basel I did the same with Philip Wolff-Windegg, editor of *Antaios*, a Jung oriented magazine. The critic Jo Excoffier interviewed me at length for radio in Geneva where I was also warmly received by the writer Walter Weideli. He was in charge of the cultural pages of the *Journal de Genève* in which he had written an enthusiastic review of *Dziady* which he had seen in 1961 in Cracow (I always carried a copy of it with me to show to people on my travels). He published my articles straightaway and it was he who chose a young actor – Eric Ducret – to come to Opole to study[28]. In Lausanne I met Antoine Apotheloz, director of the municipal theatre, Freddy Buache who directed the Cinemathèque, and René Berger, owner of the magazine *Pour l'Art* which had previously printed an article on Grotowski by Raymonde Temkine. Everywhere I went I made the obligatory visit to the various newspapers and magazines with the intention of placing an article or getting them to interview me.

My missionary work efforts were concentrated on Paris. The house of Raymonde and Valentin Temkine was my refuge, as it also later became that of Grotowski, Flaszen, Ryszard Cieślak and Erik Veaux.

My Parisian wanderings included the elite amongst the people who counted or had the possibility of publishing information. I started by calling on Roger Caillois and Enrico Fulchignoni at UNESCO, and then Claude Lévi-Strauss at his office on the Avenue d'Iéna. In those days, to receive a messenger with semi-clandestine information from behind "the iron curtain" was something of a sensation. They were all very forthcoming. The time they devoted to me was brief, but some of them unwittingly contributed to reinforcing Grotowski's position in Poland. The aim of these visits was twofold. On the one hand I wanted to tell people inter-

[27] On the way to India by car, I passed through Milan to collect the fee which was to finance my trip. With a sad expression, Franco Quadri announced that the money was not yet available and that the publisher was not present, together with a thousand other excuses. Such was my anger that, either from pity or prudence, Franco Quadri calmed me down by advancing me half of the sum from his own pocket. From this stormy encounter a friendship was born which neither time nor personal choice have impaired. Franco became a courageous and independent critic. Not only did he continue to publish my texts on Grotowski in *Sipario*, but he also invited me and three of Odin Teatret's actors to the historic Ivrea congress in 1967. Later he personally financed from his own pocket at a loss the tour to Milan with *Ferai*, and his publishing house has also brought out some of my books.

[28] The mayor of Opole had given me a small scholarship for six months. As I already had one from the Italian government, Grotowski and I thought of giving it to a foreign student. It would have made a good impression if other foreigners besides myself gravitated around the Teatr 13 Rzędów.

ested in the world of "archetypes" about the Teatr-Laboratorium's method and, on the other, to ask them to write a letter to Grotowski expressing their interest in his research and requesting further information.

I spoke several times with Jean Jacquot of the Centre National de Recherche Scientifique and he introduced me to Denis Bablet. Then there was André Veinstein at the Bibliothèque de l'Arsénal where I deposited material on the Teatr-Laboratorium for their archives. I met the playwright François Billetdoux, René Sieffert who was a specialist in Japanese theatre, magazine editors such as Louis Pauwels (*Planète*), Maurice Nadeau (*Les Lettres Nouvelles*) and Gaëtan Picon (*Mercure de France*).

Raymonde Temkine insisted that I meet Roger Blin. I had no idea who he was and it was not a great help to learn that he was an exceptional actor and director and had collaborated with Artaud, a name I had only recently come across. He received me in his home, and I was immediately paralysed by his stutter. He stumbled over several words in the same sentence, sometimes at such length and with such force that he appeared to be having an epileptic fit. I was bewildered and unable to understand how he could possibly be an actor. However, I was told that on stage he spoke without the least difficulty. I was so embarrassed that I cannot have been very convincing.

I managed a couple of big successes. One was with Jacques Poliéri, avant-garde director and scenographer, who was editing an issue of *Architecture Aujourd'hui* on theatre space in our century. He devoted an entire page to Jerzy Gurawski's sketches and drawings for the productions of the Teatr-Laboratorium 13 Rzędów. Later, Poliéri and Grotowski attempted to invent projects in common but these were never implemented[29].

The other was a meeting with Jean Darcante, Secretary General of the ITI, the International Theatre Institute (UNESCO's non-governmental organisation concerned with theatre and dance). He published an international magazine and accepted an article of mine. Darcante's secretary, Lis Frederiksen, was Danish and, thanks to my 'Norwegian' identity, we became friends, kept up a correspondence and she turned into an effective Trojan horse during the ITI's World Congress in Warsaw in June 1963.

Raymonde Temkine paved the way for me by contacting and introducing me to many people she knew: Guy Rétoré of the Théâtre de l'Est in Paris, and Antoine Bourseiller at the Studio des Champs Elysées. Bourseiller took my visit seriously, wrote to Grotowski and met him when he came to France. He proposed that Grotowski should direct the

---

[29] See Letter 6 from Grotowski of 12 May 1964.

medieval mystery play *Le miracle de Théophile* (which never came about) and he brought him to Aix-en-Provence to give seminars when he became the director of that town's theatre.

The Scandinavian route presented no prestigious names. In Stockholm I met Öyvind Fahlström, painter and creator of happenings or K.G. Hultén, director of the Modern Museum and future director of the Pompidou Centre in Paris (it was Achille Perilli who gave me their names). There were poets such as Jess Ørnsbo in Copenhagen, and in Oslo, Jens Bjørneboe, writer and very dear friend. My meetings with critics and journalists from all over Scandinavia gave unexpected results when I founded Odin Teatret. The majority of them remembered me for my Grotowskian proselytism.

I was glad to return to Opole, to the pleasure of seeing Grotowski again and proudly show him my booty: letters, proposals, a published article or interview. In my room or at the station restaurant I told him of every person I had met, giving a detailed account of their reactions, comments, indifference or interest, the promises and the doubts. We felt as though the world was expanding. Then there was the pleasure of sharing the books bought abroad.

When people ask me today what is the most important thing Grotowski taught me, I reply that I learnt to resist, to hold out against the spirit of the time, not to let my back be broken, and to keep alive the spark which, although hidden in a far off province, would set fire to ten, a hundred, a thousand other people.

But I had absorbed a mass of knowledge during those days and months seated on a chair and watching the work at the Teatr 13 Rzędów. My lack of practical experience, of direct contact with the actors, of collaboration with musicians and scenographers seemed to me an insurmountable handicap during my first steps with Odin Teatret. However, I managed to make things work with my 'actors' who were young and without experience but had great expectations. I asked myself how Grotowski would have acted in each specific case, or else I simply copied what I had seen him do during rehearsals, as for instance:

- how to let the actor compose each action;
- how to interpret the character by means of vocal and physical effects, maintaining a continuous and coherent relationship with the text;
- how to use every word as a vocal action: not only as an intellectual tool but also as musicality capable of arousing associations in the spectator;
- how every sequence, however short, must have its own composition and logic;

- how the actors must be able to decide on which formal element the attention of the spectator is to be concentrated, whether on a physical or a vocal effect, on one or other particular part of the body, on themselves or on some distant point;
- how to create a 'polemic' by subverting the value of a physical or vocal action through the simultaneous introduction of expressive elements which contradict that action;
- how to get the actor to carry out a multiple composition passing rapidly from one character to another;
- how to induce the actor to become a multiform Proteus, a shaman who can change from a living person into an object, slipping instantaneously from one reality to another, vanishing or flying *before the very eyes of the spectators*;
- how to treat the costumes and the props in such a way that they have a life and character of their own and constantly create an opposition between the actors and their actions.

I learnt that the formal aspects are fundamental, but they overflow into virtuosity and risk producing a trained monkey, an actor who is a puppet in the hands of the director. Only the actor's inner commitment can guard against this danger. The opposite pole to technique is psychic and mental discipline. Personal motivation in theatre, whether conscious or not, is confession which emerges from regions deep within the artist.

The years spent at the Teatr 13 Rzędów made me absorb a theatre vision and a way of living it, both intellectually and emotionally, as technique and aspiration. They provided me with a terminology that enabled me to have a dialogue with myself and my actors, a language which was mine, ours, personal and fleeting, which supplanted the usual or obvious categories of the discourse on theatre. Fate had smiled on me. I had encountered a master and had devoured him whole. I kept him inside me. In moments of joy I embraced him and in times of difficulty and danger he gave me support.

Theatre is constituted by roots which grow in a particular place, but it also consists of seeds carried by the wind and following the routes of birds. Dreams, ideas and techniques travel around with individuals, and each encounter deposits pollen, a promise of fertility. The fruit ripens through persistent toil, blind necessity and a spirit of improvisation, and contains the seeds of new rebellious truths.

The Value of a Bus

For thirty years chance has preserved a postcard which still adorns my writing desk. It is a colour reproduction of a project by Wincenty Drabik for the scenography of Juliusz Osterwa's production of *The Constant Prince* in 1918. The Polish postal service printed it on the occasion of the Tenth Congress of the ITI, the International Theatre Institute, which was held in Warsaw from 8-15 June, 1963. It is one of those pictures which evokes premonitions and memories because Osterwa was an important example for Grotowski and because, a few years later, Grotowski's own *Constant Prince* was to project him onto the international scene. Furthermore, during the course of that Tenth Congress of the ITI his current production – *Doctor Faustus* – provoked, for the first time, an international reaction amongst the fifty or so foreigners who saw it in Poland.

The ITI was a prestigious organisation and the Poles were very proud of the decision to hold its congress in Warsaw, considering it a sign of appreciation of their theatre. Bohdan Korzeniewski, my ex-teacher from the theatre school, was also the Polish representative with the international committee in Paris and he was responsible for the organisation of the congress.

The Poles had prepared an excellent programme for the more than two hundred delegates from all over the world. But on reading it through, Grotowski and I noticed that the theatre from Opole was not even mentioned. Something had to be done about it.

The Teatr-Laboratorium 13 Rzędów could not go on tour to Warsaw because nobody would have been prepared to host it. Another solution was needed. A base had to be found as close as possible to the capital and as many delegates as possible diverted towards our theatre. We decided to take *Doctor Faustus* to Łódź which was about a hundred kilometres from Warsaw and far enough for it not to appear that we were attaching ourselves to the congress. Łódź had a flourishing cultural life and could probably provide enough spectators for the ten planned performances. I was to act as a fifth column, going to Warsaw and mingling with the delegates at the congress. Circumstances would decide how this was to be done.

The congress took place in the Palace of Culture, a huge building in the Stalinist style, which looked like a gigantic wedding cake. In the vast entrance hall I approached the groups of participants to hear which language they were speaking. I first identified some Swedes, and then some Norwegians, joining in with their conversation and explaining that I was studying theatre in Poland. As casually as possible I showed off my local knowledge, placing myself at their disposal as to information on where to buy the best souvenirs, which restaurants could be recommended, and which performances were a MUST. Soon I was more or less adopted by the dozen or so Scandinavians and attached myself to them as though I were part of one of their delegations.

This is where Lis Frederiksen appeared, Jean Darcante's Danish secretary, whom I had met in Paris. She arrived, smiling, together with an English girl called Judy Jones who was also an ITI secretary. Lis complained about the Polish organisers who had promised her a French and English speaking shorthand typist, but none had turned up. 'If you have the money, I'll find you one', I told her. So I rang Adriana Salvagni, an Italian girl with a scholarship who lived in my student hostel. Adriana (who later became a career diplomat) arrived and was immediately taken on: access to the ITI secretariat was assured. That evening I invited Lis to go dancing at a nightspot in the old town. She brought Judy along too and I arrived with an artist friend and a scenographer. That evening was for fraternisation; the next day work would begin.

Talking to various people and listening to the first day's discussions, I realised that the one person who simply had to see *Doctor Faustus* was Jean Julien. He was the director of the Théâtre des Nations, the festival which every year invited the best international productions to Paris. I went up to him during one of the breaks, surrounded as he was by many people, and let fall a couple of remarks about Polish theatre and what a pity it was that they couldn't see the most interesting things, such as the theatre at the home of the poet Miron Białoszewski, Piwnica's performances in Cracow, a few of the student theatres and Grotowski's Teatr-Laboratorium 13 Rzędów. Explaining how Poland was the country of paradoxes with its gloomy official shell and its audacious creativity, the socialist puritanism and the Slavonic *joie de vivre*, I offered to take him on a tour of Warsaw by night and show him the nocturnal mysteries of a socialist capital. But I made a condition: that he should come to a performance on the outskirts of Warsaw that lasted barely an hour. Julien accepted. I rang Teresa Ziemska, a friend who was a cellist. I told her that she simply had to go out with me and Julien, explaining the agreement I had with him to come and see Grotowski's performance. Teresa, who had infinite patience with my passion for the Teatr-Laboratorium, did not refuse.

That evening, when the day's sessions were over, Julien arrived together with Emile Biasini, the representative for the French Ministry of Culture who financed the Théâtre des Nations. He wanted to come too. We were just leaving when we bumped into Judy, the ITI's English secretary, and Julien invited her as well. The carefully planned *tête-à-tête* between me and Julien in the company of a Polish *jeune fille en fleur* was turning into a tourist outing!

We went to a popular restaurant in Mokotów, with a demoniacal orchestra, where everybody drank, danced and sang in chorus – a mixture of a New Year's Eve atmosphere and *après nous le déluge*. Suddenly the orchestra struck up with *Czerwone maki na Montecassino*, the song recalling the heroism of the Polish soldiers in 1944 in their conquest of the fortified German position in Montecassino, Italy ('years will pass and centuries will vanish, but traces of days gone by will remain and the poppies of Montecassino will be redder than ever because they spring from Polish blood') and everyone stood up in silence, as a sign of respect and pride, until suddenly the whole place exploded once again into dancing and music.

We moved on to a couple of other student haunts, a jazz club and finally to the Kongresowa, a huge restaurant with a grotesque strip-tease show. A truly popular and socialist night out, with Teresa straight out of *The Divine Comedy* as an exemplary Beatrice/Virgil guiding Jean Julien and Emile Biasini who exclaimed in astonishment or squabbled over politics and finance, while Judy felt unwell after a couple of glasses of vodka. It was not a boring night and when I accompanied them to the Hotel Francuski, Julien thanked me, reminding me that the following evening we would go to the theatre together.

I had spoken with other delegates and some of them had expressed the wish to see this Grotowski. I had to organise a rapid form of transport if we were to get to the performance on time. I had thought of taking Julien by taxi to Łódź. But what would I do with the others who were now more than a dozen? I rang Jerzy Kotliński whom I had met in September 1962 in Kołobrzeg on the Baltic Sea, together with his wife Zofia. I had been spending a week there as guest of a student organisation, whereas they were on holiday. They were party members, loyal and convinced communists, totally lacking in cynicism and with an extraordinary human quality. He was the director of a jam factory in Saska Kępa, a part of Warsaw on the other side of the river Vistula. I explained the situation to him. I was looking for a bus that would take about twenty people, and I needed it that same evening at half past five. Could he get hold of one for me from his factory? Yes, it could be done. It was only a question of money and he mentioned a sum. It was beyond my possibilities. There was a long silence and then the consolatory voice of Jerzy Kotliński: 'not to worry, Eugeniusz, I'll lend it to you'. Such was the generosity of Polish friendship.

So it was that at five o'clock in the afternoon the miracle happened: a state owned bus which, in theory, could not be used for private purposes, was parked in front of the Palace of Culture where the congress was being held. About twenty people boarded the bus: Eduardo Manet, Director from the National Theatre in Havana who later became a well known author in France; Hubert Gignoux, Director of the Centre Dramatique de l'Est in Strasbourg; the Finnish critic Kasja Krook; the Italian critic Raul Radice (*Il Tempo*); the American journalist Henry Popkin (*The New York Times*); the young Finnish director Kristin Olsoni; the Flemish playwrights Tone Brulin and Jan Christiaens; the Australian playwright Alan Seymour (*Plays and Players*, London); the Swedish directors Ingrid Luterkort and Palle Brunius; the Icelandic director Sveinn Einarsson; the Canadian director Jean Louis Roux; the Belgian actor and director René Hainaux and the British critic Ossia Trilling. Those are the names I remember, and they are people who remained in contact with me for many years. Apart from them there were about ten to fifteen other people, including Judy, who wanted to see this theatre about which I never stopped talking. They were all on board the bus, but Julien had not arrived. I was desperate. We had to leave in order to be on time for the performance. I rushed inside the building, asking everyone if they had seen him. Suddenly I saw him coming out of a room. Apologising, he explained that he was in a meeting with Jean Darcante, Michel Saint-Denis (the famous director, ex-pupil of Copeau, and one of the Copiaus), Bohdan Korzeniewski and some others. He could not get away for another half hour. I had to make an immediate decision: whether or not to go without Julien.

I went over to the driver of the bus, gave him the address in Łódź and told my guests that I would catch up with them in no time. I made a deal with a taxi driver and we settled down to wait patiently. Finally Julien arrived together with Michel Saint-Denis and his wife Suria who had also decided to come along to the performance in the 'suburbs'. I promised an extra tip to the driver if he reached Łódź before eight o'clock. A two hour car trip can sometimes seem like an eternity. At first Julien and Saint-Denis were puzzled, then impatient, then clearly irritated. Where was I taking them? When we arrived, the performance had already begun and the stage hand, who obviously knew me very well, would not let us in. Orders were orders for everyone, even me. Should I strangle him? I dragged my guests, who by now had given up resisting their hothead of a guide, up a staircase and on to a balcony overlooking the scene. From there we watched *Doctor Faustus*.

After the performance, Julien's face had changed. So too had that of Michel Saint-Denis and all the other foreign guests. Their expressions were luminous, marvelling, like children who have seen snow for the first time. I took them to another room where Grotowski and the actors joined us. There were many questions. In the bus on the way back there was silence. It was late and I was exhausted. I rested my head on Judy's shoulder; perhaps I slept.

The following day, at the morning session of the congress, Jean Julien stood up and thanked the Polish hosts for giving him the chance to see a remarkable performance: *Doctor Faustus* by the Teatr-Laboratorium 13 Rzędów. Amazement all round. Then Eduardo Manet got up. His words carried great prestige. He came from Cuba, a socialist country, and furthermore he directed the National Theatre. He too praised the performance at length. The playwrights Tone Brulin and Jan Christiaens presented an official motion: 'The Flemish delegation considers that yesterday evening in Łódź it was confronted with the type of theatre which will contribute towards the liberation of an art that has long been dominated by a conventional way of thinking[30].'

For a moment, the congress hall became the Tower of Babel. The Poles could not understand what had happened, and the other delegates asked why they too had not been invited. Korzeniewski, the perfect diplomat, gave nothing away. Particularly impressive was the capacity of Julien, Manet, Tone Brulin and Jan Christiaens to formulate what I had told them about the financial and political difficulties of the 13 Rzędów, in a way that was 'politically correct' for the communists.

Those thirty or so participants from the ITI congress marked a turning point for Grotowski. On their return home they wrote long and enthusiastic articles in magazines and newspapers. The seed had been sown for a tour to the Théâtre des Nations. Julien would definitely bring the Teatr-Laboratorium 13 Rzędów to Paris. Unfortunately he retired as director at the end of that year. However, thanks to the tireless struggle of Raymonde and Valentin Temkine and the comments of the new 'witnesses' such as Gignoux and Saint-Denis, Jean Louis Barrault, who took over, continued the efforts to conquer the resistance of the Polish authorities. In June 1966, three years after the Warsaw congress, Grotowski and his actors

---

[30] Tone Brulin and Jan Christiaens published the entire motion in Amsterdam, thanking "Grotowski, whose efforts, together with those of his companions, were of the greatest importance for Dramatic Art in the world". And they commented: "What these young actors are doing is the consequence of an attitude to life and of an aesthetic consciousness, as well as of a training lasting many months, perhaps years. The communist regime has astonished us with its cultural politics which generously subsidises this theatre that is directly inspired by the ideas of Craig, Meyerhold and Artaud. At last we have seen these theories become reality. Something that seemed impossible has come about."

presented *The Constant Prince* in Paris.

After the ITI congress I remained in Warsaw to settle the pressing problem of my debts. The sort of life I had been leading during that period – travelling, inviting people out, 'hiring' a bus, going about by taxi – was not tenable on my student scholarship. I sold everything I had that could be sold, my trumpet which had known the Chopin conservatoire, jeans and nylon shirts which were rare in Poland at the time. My Polish friends lent me considerable sums and waited patiently to be repaid.

I was in a particular state of mind; on the one hand the elation of recent victory and the joy of seeing the enthusiasm of so many important people for the 13 Rzędów; and on the other, a sense of anti-climax, of disorientation and an incapacity to see ahead. My scholarship had come to an end and with it my residence permit. I had to leave Poland by the end of June. My studies were not finished and I had not the least experience as a director. I had spent two and a half years sitting on a chair observing the work of others or else in frantic motion, like a Tibetan prayer wheel whose mantras were the theories of Grotowski.

After the Łódź tour the Teatr-Laboratorium 13 Rzędów had returned to Opole. I went too, to say my goodbyes to the actors, Flaszen and Grotowski. The sadness which pervaded me turned into astonishment. Grotowski was not there. Nobody knew where he was. I left Poland without seeing him[31].

I had told Judy Jones, the ITI secretary who had helped me at the congress, about my wish to return to India. I had already been there in 1956 by sea, but now I wanted to do the journey over land. She had a small Fiat 600 and would also like to make the trip. We decided to go in her car. The fact that I could not drive did not worry us unduly. I would learn along the way: there were plenty of deserts to cross.

I returned to Oslo to prepare for the trip. Judy wrote to me that the journey was impossible with her Fiat. Everyone had advised her against it, so she had bought a second-hand Land Rover which we would be able to resell on our return at virtually no loss. I convinced a friend of mine, Hans Jacob Mørdre, to come with us. He was an architect and interested in Indian philosophy. He also knew how to drive. We arranged to meet in Istanbul. I left for England where Judy and I loaded our few belongings and plenty of tinned food into the Land Rover. After crossing the English Channel, we headed towards Milan to collect the fee from *Sipario. A passage to India*: the way opened up before me – it was a long avenue in the centre of Milan.

---

[31] See letter 1 from Grotowski of 10 July 1963.

First Flashback

It was in 1955 in Oslo that, not quite twenty years old, I read a book by Romain Rolland entitled *Ramakrishna*. I discovered that in the last century in Bengal a peasant's son, a devotee of Kali, had become a monk and had had a series of illuminations. He had contributed to a revival of religious fervour at a moment when a great philosophical, literary, political and social reawakening was in progress under the central figure of Ram Mohum Roy and three generations of the Tagore family. The last, Rabindranath, the poet who had been awarded the Nobel Prize in 1913, was about twenty years younger than Ramakrishna.

Ramakrishna had spent most of his life in a temple a few kilometres from Calcutta and, in addition to Hinduism, he had experienced other forms of religion. It had created a scandal when, for a time, he had practised Muslim devotions, he who was a priest of Kali, the Mother. During another period he allowed himself to be imbued by the religion of Christ. He said that the various religions were like people of different languages who draw water from the river: each uses its own word to indicate the contents of the pitcher. The pitchers, too, are different but the substance is the same.

I can't say why, but I felt a yearning to go to Dakshineswar where Ramakrishna's temple stood, on the banks of the Ganges, built for him by a rich widow of low cast. I longed to tread those same steps which, according to Romain Rolland, Ramakrishna used to descend every morning to the river's edge to perform his ablutions.

I had no money. In 1955, going to India seemed an impossibility. As for the theatre, it had not yet even entered my mind. For me, India was those religions or philosophies which had fascinated me.

I didn't give up, and finally succeeded in getting a job on a Norwegian merchant ship. It was called *Talabot* and was bound for the Far East. We passed through the Suez Canal, arrived in Aden, continued to Colombo, Cochin, Madras, Chittagong. Then Calcutta. One morning, very early, I went to Dakshineswar and saw those steps. I too descended them to the water's edge.

Then I went back to my dirty, oily job in the deafening machine room of the *Talabot*, and to the seasickness of the return journey on the rough monsoon seas.

In Search of Theatre

Seven years later I was again travelling towards India, in a second-hand car which I didn't know how to drive. This time I wanted to learn something professionally useful. I was searching for 'Indian theatre'. In New Delhi I would finally become acquainted with it.

I was advised to meet Ebrahim Alkazi at the National School of Drama. But there, to my surprise, I found myself hearing and watching the same things that they taught at the Warsaw theatre school.

Somebody said to me: 'Why don't you go to Bombay? There you will find Adi Marzban, a writer who does some interesting theatre'. More days of driving. But in Bombay too I only found plays taken from the English tradition and popular farces.

Then someone suggested: 'Why not go down south? There you really will find something quite unique!'. He assured me that *kathakali* would not disappoint me. He was from Kerala.

So once again Judy climbed behind the wheel of the Land Rover and after crossing the whole of India, we arrived at the Kathakali Kalamandalam, in the village of Cheruthuruty in Kerala.

What I saw in Kerala is engraved for ever in my memory. The children were admitted to the school at the age of nine or ten. They started at dawn. Still numb from sleep, they began on their own to repeat again and again the laborious *kathakali* postures and steps. They were friendly and curious. They became my companions.

Even more than the beauty of the performances, it was my own incapacity to understand that surprised me. Why was I, a European spectator, so bewitched by these actors when I could neither understand the story they were telling, nor the meaning of their message, nor their language or the conventions? What was it that made me follow every gesture, every step, dance or deaf-mute dialogue of these actors? Was it their technique that kept me spellbound during an entire night, seated on the ground amongst a crowd who slept or continually got up to stretch their legs, or to eat or drink?

These questions constituted the true influence on me of *kathakali*. For years and years they have remained alive, and have then reappeared in other contexts, leading me towards an attempt at an answer that I have called Theatre Anthropology.

In mid-December I returned to my mother's home in Rome only to discover that the Italian government had, for the fourth time, renewed my scholarship to Poland. I sent a telegram to Grotowski and set off immediately for Opole.

The Friendless Hamlet

We had a lot to tell each other. In my room or in the station restaurant

Grotowski brought me up to date with everything that had happened during my absence. Zbigniew Cynkutis, who had played Kordian and then Faustus, had left the theatre and two new actors had been engaged. The situation had not improved, political pressures had become intolerable and to make matters worse, money was short because the subsidies had been suspended. He explained how far they had come with rehearsals for the new production, *Studium o Hamlecie*, 'Study on Hamlet', why he had chosen that particular text, how he had gone about extracting the archetype and what was the basis for the dialectic of apotheosis and derision. I described my trip to him and the performances I had seen, and I told him about *kathakali* and the religious ceremonies I had attended in Iran, Pakistan and India. I had started to write down my observations on *kathakali* and had adapted some 'exercises' for the training of the Teatr-Laboratorium's actors. I had taken a series of photographs of the *kathakali* children. They were doubtless far more suggestive and eloquent than my descriptions could ever be.

Grotowski divided his time between meetings with the authorities in Opole or Warsaw and rehearsals of *Studium o Hamlecie*, based on the Shakespeare text and an essay by Stanisław Wyspiański. Zygmunt Molik was the protagonist. I arrived at an advanced stage in the process. One could already glimpse the dramaturgical structure, the conception of the director and the actors' achievements. I sat down on my usual chair, faithful to my task of assistant/observer. When the production was presented publicly in mid-March I wrote an article which was never published because *Studium o Hamlecie* was immediately taken off the repertoire. I am including it here in its entirety as testimony of a production which is often ignored in Grotowski's artistic career:

Hamlet at the Teatr-Laboratorium 13 Rzędów (1964)
Who is Hamlet? A psychopath? A cynic? A spineless intellectual? A naïf? Or a sort of Arturo Ui who terrorises the court? Perhaps he is possessed by absolute ethical categories? Perhaps he is the only one who rejects the moral pragmatism of daily survival. He shows signs of Freudian complexes and an inability to conform? But is he solitary by vocation or by chance? Is he capable of action and merely pretending not to be? He seems to be deceiving himself, but at the same time he is very clever at deceiving others. Is he driven by an impulse for self-destruction? Is he acting a part in order to hide his vacuity? Is he consumed by a desire for revenge? Or is he infatuated by his own intellectuality?

Hamlet is alone, he isolates himself and he is isolated by others. Every attempt at contact fails. The very fact that he exists condemns him to be an outcast. But how can we explain his solitude and isolation in the surrounding community? What significance should we attribute to his detachment as an outsider? And who are the insiders?

Hamlet is the 'Jew' and the others are the 'goyim', the Gentiles. He is different, the others are normal. He philosophises, the others live. He acts with caution, the others act without hesitation. He dreams of doing, while the others do. No possibility of contact, no tolerance exists between the 'Jew' and the 'group'. Each regards the other as a danger. Hamlet is the 'Jew' in a community, whatever sense we attach to the word: ideological, religious, social, aesthetic, moral or sexual. He is different and is therefore a risk. Every group needs to have its 'Jew' for the sake of self-definition, in order to reinforce the awareness of its own value and for the well being of one's own convictions.

*

Study on Hamlet is the title of the latest production directed by Jerzy Grotowski at his Teatr-Laboratorium in Opole. Shakespeare's text mingles with comments by Stanisław Wyspiański, Poland's great symbolist playwright, poet, director and painter. In his book of the same title as the production, Wyspiański concluded that it was impossible to represent the story of the Danish prince because of the vast number of possible interpretations, and above all for the radical transformation it would have been subjected to in adapting the story to the customs of the country 'on the banks of the river Vistula'.

Grotowski takes up this double affirmation and makes it the main pivot of the production. The impossibility of playing Hamlet presents the opportunity to unmask the attitude of a community. This impossibility, however, does not depend on the interpretative multiplicity of the drama, but on the feeling of 'impotence' inherent in the national character itself. The same theme of 'national impotence' had been dealt with in literature by Wyspiański (Wesele, The Wedding), by Gombrowicz (Ferdydurke) and by Mrożek (Indyk, The Turkey). Thus all the peripeties of the Danish prince happen on the banks of the Vistula. 'The action takes place in Poland, that is, nowhere'. The characters are the peasants of a King Ubu who, although invisible, is embodied in each one of them. Hamlet has become a rural drama, and the protagonist is the village Jew.

So, here we are at the tavern. Everybody drinks and sings a drunken song in chorus. Now and then the peasants make an effort to play Shakespeare's text, do a rough outline of some scenes, and then withdraw declaring that it is an impossible task. They relapse into their basic vital attitude: drinking and fornicating. They are mean and brutal, always in a group, ready to tear each other to pieces. The 'elementary pleasures of life', alcohol which gives enthousiasmos *and love which gives* kalagathon, *are merely an expression of continuous excess for these troglodytic beings. Hamlet participates in their permanent orgy, discoursing upon human nature. He attempts to merge with them, to approach a woman, to sing in chorus. In vain.*

The king needs soldiers. The cunning peasants enrol their 'Jew' in the army. Still philosophising and planning to avenge the death of his father, Hamlet/Ahasverus is lined up and marches towards the battle. 'Isaac Babel in the cavalry brigade' could be the title of his wartime peregrinations: the Jew from Odessa amongst the Cossacks, the experts in pogroms. The true warriors mock the intellectual for his spectacles, his ineptitude on horseback, his sensitivity which prevents him from giving a dying comrade-in-arms the coup de grâce to cut short his suffering.

Hamlet is trained, humiliated, toughened. Then he trains, humiliates, toughens others in his turn. The time for action arrives. Sadism, hate, threats fill the space. The soldier-peasants throw themselves at imaginary enemies. The acrid smell of sweat mingles with the frenzied shouts of the murderers and the groans of the dying. Bodies roll on the ground, get to their feet again only to fall back, writhing. Rape and torture, cruelty and bestiality reveal the face of homo miles, *the military man. Hamlet takes refuge in an interminable monologue: to be or not to be? He is present, as a distant witness, while the actors confront an imaginary adversary (lurking in the subconscious?) with a savage violence which does not even spare their own bodies. He wants to remain outside, not to surrender to the collective madness. The others grab him and oblige him to torture, to 'act', to participate in the brutality and contempt which unites the group. The march is resumed. The 'cavalry brigade' moves on to other exploits.*

After the baptism of fire, Hamlet returns to the village. There he finds the peasants, identical to the soldiers he has just left, drinking, singing and making love. Nobody recognises him. Only a dog welcomes him back. The meeting with his mother ends with the murder of a peasant, Polonius. Dragging the body behind him, Hamlet takes refuge in the public baths. Gathered in the sauna, the peasants fight and squirm like a disgusting monster to which the nudity of the actors lends a bestial physiology. Their erotic games reflect the despiritualisation of man, the animality. Hamlet alone, completely dressed, washes himself with a distinguished meticulousness. Tragedy strikes like a thunderbolt. Polonius' body is discovered, and Ophelia dies in the course of an erotic game. The peasants are astonished and terrified in the face of death's mystery, and their nakedness becomes the very symbol of the human condition and anguish when pushed to extreme limits. Those same people who behaved like animals on heat rediscover a form of humanity made up of prayers and laments, invocations and religious fervour. Where is the true profile of man? What is the truth? Only a few moments before, these creatures were prey to instincts that we observed with shame and disgust.

Once more the king summons his peasants to war. Hamlet returns to his 'cavalry brigade' which the awareness of imminent death surrounds with an aura of nobility. Now the battalions advance, in formation, impassive, transfigured, towards the tomb of History:

Mother of God, blessed
Virgin Mary
Kyrie Eleyson.

This religious litany, with which Polish warriors once invoked divine protection when facing the Teutonic knights in Grünwald and the Turks outside Vienna, accompanies the peasant-soldiers on their march towards the battlefield.

The king is the gravedigger. As the troops file past, he recognises his soldiers but speaks of them in the past tense: they are already corpses. Before the fate awaiting them, these men do not hesitate, they do not object: reasoning makes man weak. They take action and pay for it with their lives. And Hamlet?

He recites monologues: the brutality and the horror of war act as a stimulant on his brain. He wants to transmit his rational and humanistic message to the marching hordes. They spit in his face. He cries, throwing himself at their feet to stop them. They trample on him. He shouts, invokes, pleads, weeps and questions whilst the battalions

Mother of God, blessed
Virgin Mary
Kyrie Eleyson

charge towards their destiny of greatness. His reason wants to suffocate the myth that animates these people. He wants to strip them of their impulses, of their desire for submission, to give themselves and, in so doing, to act.

Hamlet is right: such a death is meaningless; war is barbaric, an obliteration of all value and dignity. Hamlet is wrong: there is no place for discussion when the only way out is action. The battlefield is littered with the dead. The soldier-peasants preferred to be corpses rather than live as such. After his efforts to halt the massacre, Hamlet crouches on the ground. In a frail voice, he hums a Yiddish song. He wails like a child: he laments his inadequacy at saving the others and his fear of marching with them. As if to mock him, a drunken song rises from the corpses. The king-gravedigger kneels down among the bodies of his soldiers and sings the Kyrie Eleyson. The lights go out on the drama of Hamlet, and the country 'on the banks of the Vistula' returns to darkness.

Let us imagine a festering and fetid wound, covered by a white bandage. Suddenly the bandage is stripped off and the scab gets torn away. Pain mingles with disgust at the pus and the blood. That is Grotowski's Study on Hamlet. He has removed the bandage which adorns and controls our conscience and has laid bare the Eros and the Thanatos rooted in the subconscious of the individual and collective imagination. It is a terrifying and horrible vivisection that smells of sweat, blood and sperm – a merciless vision of the individual and the group swept along by instinct. It is a transfiguration of the Shakespearian substance. The violence, passion and meanness of human beings are revealed to us among flashes and visions that appeal to our collective memory.

The actors' performance is a form of blackmail; it is not daily behaviour, but a physiology of an extraordinary state: sexual climax, agon, torture, rape. Inarticulate shouts and aberrant raucous voices gush forth, controlled and yet free, from a psycho-technique which permeates every element in the composition of the actors. Their performance does not convince, it terrifies, disturbs, brutally shakes the defenceless spectator. The nudity and perspiration, the contorted faces and convulsed bodies remind us of a reality that is so close, so inherent in us. There is one single semblance of light: the violence and bestiality of the peasant-soldiers are sublimated in an incandescent spiritual force in the final scene. Hamlet continues to spit out reflections on the necessity for action, and talks of wanting to remain with the peasants, sharing their impotence and not outliving them. How can one feel like a victim if there are no longer executioners? But his form of impotence consists in the incapacity to feel, live and die with the others. Because he is unable to, and because the others do not want him to.

Balancing between these two attitudes, the spectator sinks into a third form of impotence: that of the short-sighted and pragmatic humanist who refuses to recognise what king Ubu's peasants and the Jew-Hamlet have unmasked: the miles, *the military man, slumbering within each one of us.*

Studium o Hamlecie, which overflows with excesses by the actors and flashes of geniality by the director, existential revolt and political dissent, seems to me to contain the germs of the diverse facets of future European theatre. But in March 1964, this eruption was a slap in the face for everyone, friends and enemies alike; it escaped the comprehension and the sensitivity of the Teatr-Laboratorium 13 Rzędów's supporters and shook the criteria and the norms of Polish socialism. The themes of Grotowski's previous productions were to be found here, carried to their utmost limits, all with a politically explicit subtext, and all connected with

Poland's history: the intellectual who wants to act (*Dziady* and *Kordian*), the individual who sets himself up against a stronger will (*Doctor Faustus*), the community which is infuriated against the *outsider* who wants to remain loyal to his principles. These themes reappear in *The Constant Prince*, in which the intensity of the rejection of a society and its values are embodied by the actors in a shocking way, in particular by Ryszard Cieślak.

It is understandable that the Polish authorities were irritated. Even Grotowski's allies raised objections putting forward aesthetic, technical or dramaturgical arguments and making unfavourable comparisons between *Studium o Hamlecie* and *Akropolis* or *Doctor Faustus*. I loved this production as an uncle might love a stillborn nephew. I was not present during the period of gestation, and when it came into the world, my reaction was one of bewilderment in the presence of such violence. I missed the touching moments when personal wounds were laid bare. Nevertheless, even today, scraps of those scenes and fragments of those songs live in my memory and visit me during my work at the Odin.

This production must also have aroused conflicting reactions in Grotowski. Today he maintains that it was a fundamental stage in his method in order for the actor to attain the 'total act' as incarnated by Ryszard Cieślak in the role of the constant prince. But I believe that, at the time and over the next few years, Grotowski did not consider *Studium o Hamlecie* to be a successful production. In April 1965, on the last page of the programme of *The Constant Prince*, the 'most important productions' presented by the Teatr-Laboratorium 13 Rzędów are listed: *Cain* (1960), *Mystery Bouffe* (1960), *Shakuntala* (1961), *Dziady* (1961), *Kordian* (1962), *Akropolis* (1962), *Doctor Faustus* (1963). *Study on Hamlet*, the 'Jew' of the family, is passed over in silence.

The cat and mouse game was coming to an end. The situation was no longer one of ideological and aesthetic conflict, or of incomprehension on the part of theatre circles or the critics. By now we were in a state of siege, with the threat by the authorities to close definitively the Teatr-Laboratorium 13 Rzędów hanging over our heads. Once again we had to demonstrate that such a decision would be a grave error and would have far reaching repercussions abroad. We had to make the most of our international contacts and create new ones, consolidate the public image of Grotowski's value and influence.

I worked day and night. The result was a booklet in French of about fifty pages, with the rather grandiloquent title: *The theatre-laboratory 13 Rzędów in Opole or theatre as collective self-penetration*. It included a couple of my long articles, signed, and another ten or so that were also mine but bore no signature, as well as texts by Ludwik Flaszen, Raymonde Temkine, Kristin Olsoni, Roland Grünberg and excerpts from articles by the delegates who had seen *Doctor Faustus* in Łódź. I again took up the laborious pursuit of money. This booklet was also able to be printed and to escape censorship thanks to friends and bribes. I particularly remember Tadeusz Jackowski, a graphic artist friend of mine, knocking on the door of my hotel room in Cracow early one morning with the money that was still lacking[32].

I filled my suitcase with booklets and left on a lightning trip to Paris.

In the meantime the Polish Ministry of Culture decided to send a commission to Opole to evaluate the activity of the Teatr-Laboratorium 13 Rzędów and decide on its future. Bohdan Korzeniewski was among the members of the commission, and also Zbigniew Raszewski, editor of the magazine *Pamiętnik Teatralny*. I wonder what they must have thought on seeing *Studium o Hamlecie* in which the protagonist is an intellectual who speaks Polish with a Jewish inflection, among peasants who spit on him while singing patriotic songs from the Armia Krajowa[33]. Raszewski, who served in the Armia Krajowa, must certainly have been disconcerted.

Grotowski had many friends in the commission and Korzeniewski himself did not draw back when it came to defending him. The Ministry of Culture was informed that the theatre in Opole possessed great qualities and merited support.

So for the moment the threat of closure was kept at bay[34].

---

[32] In 1967 Tadeusz Jackowski came to Holstebro where Odin Teatret had organised an exhibition of his work at the Museum of Art. At the same time he designed the poster for *Kaspariana*, our second production, as well as the cover of a book being published by our theatre: *Towards a Poor Theatre*.

[33] The Armia Krajowa (National Army) was the resistance movement against the Germans led by the Polish governent in exile in London. There was also another resistance movement, the Armia Ludowa (People's Army), under the command of the communists who took power after the war thanks to the presence in Poland of the Soviet army. *Ashes and Diamonds*, Wajda's film which I had seen in Oslo in 1959 and which had made such an impression on me that I had decided to study in Poland, was about the civil war between the factions of these two movements.

[34] Bohdan Korzeniewski, in *Sława i infamia* (Fame and Infamy), Widawnictwo Literackie, Cracow 1989, a weighty interview of over 300 pages with Małgorzata Szejnert, names Grotowski only once (p. 201): 'They wanted to get rid of Grotowski, but whether only from Opole or altogether I do not remember. In any case, he telephoned to *Pamiętnik Teatralny* which had always been on his side. As far back as 1964 Raszewski had published an article on the Teatr-Laboratorium 13 Rzędów. Grotowski telephoned to say that a commission from the ministry was coming to Opole and that he expected the worst. We had problems in obtaining travel allowances, but in the end Rusinek gave the order that we should receive

Persona Non Grata

The situation nevertheless remained serious. On my return from Paris I had followed the work of the commission from the sidelines. Now it was necessary to leave once more in order to achieve the impossible abroad: invitations or at least support. The reactions of communist intellectuals in particular could be important, and especially those of the Italians who enjoyed considerable prestige. In this way their favourable opinions could be brought to bear against the intransigent Poles. Scandinavia was also included in this trip.

It was becoming increasingly difficult to place articles about Grotowski. I looked for new formulas. In Copenhagen I approached the magazine *Vindrosen* and proposed an issue devoted exclusively to Polish culture. Jess Ørnsbo, one of the editors and a well-known avant-garde poet, knew Polish well and was a Witkacy specialist. It was easy enough to agree on the quality of Polish artistic life, but when I suggested devoting a whole issue of the magazine to it, and in addition proposed collaborating with the Norwegian magazine *Vinduet* and the Swedish *Bonniers litterära magasin*, Jess Ørnsbo burst out laughing and accused me of being hopelessly naive. Each of those magazines, he explained, wanted to distinguish itself from the others and would never fraternise in the name of Polish culture.

He questioned me about myself. I began to talk about Grotowski, his theories, his productions. I had also written a book and had with me the

---

them. I went by car with Raszewski, Timoszewicz and Wysiński, and we arrived just in time for the discussion. Konstanty Puzyna and a few other people also arrived with the intention of defending the theatre. The head of the ministerial commission was Jerzy Jasieński, director of Theatre Affairs at the Ministry of Culture. Grotowski's self-defence was clumsy. He was foundering. I asked for a break and went in search of the regional representative of the communist party. I told him that things of immense importance were happening in that room. When Opole was German, it was an isolated province on the confines of the nation, a place with no culture of its own. Now Opole had its own theatre of international repute. The loss of this theatre, the disappearance of such an obvious Polish influence, would be a major political error. In this way Grotowski earned a little time, and later the judicious and independent president of Wrocław, Professor Iwaszkiewicz, invited him and the ensemble to his town. I certainly helped Grotowski whom I appreciated but, for my part, experiments outside the realm of traditional theatre did not interest me. I asked Grotowski: "Well, *Pan*, this time you succeeded, but what will you do in seven years' time?" He looked surprised: "Why seven?" "Because all theatres with new ideas lead a dog's life. A pedigree dog - a Pekinese. Their life is short. Then they are transformed into a caricature of themselves".'

Korzeniewski's story is interesting for various reasons. It shows how a friendly orientated magazine like *Pamiętnik Teatralny* published material on Grotowski only in 1964; how the fate of the Teatr-Laboratorium 13 Rzędów was decided on the basis of political arguments; and also how the reconstruction of the past is profoundly subjective. Grotowski, in fact, bestows upon Konstanty Puzyna the role of 'saviour' of his theatre. Cfr. Letter 6 note 45.

typed manuscript in French: *The Psycho-Dynamic Theatre*[35] (which was published in Italy under the title *In Search of Lost Theatre*). He asked if he might borrow it, promising to send it on to me in Oslo in a couple of days. It was my only copy, and I handed it over hesitantly. In Oslo I promptly received the manuscript together with a letter from Jess Ørnsbo asking permission to publish fragments of it in the next issue of *Vindrosen*. This he did, adding eight pages of photos. The impact in Denmark was considerable. It made such an impression on some artists and theatre scholars that they were sympathetic towards Odin Teatret when it moved to Holstebro in 1966.

As was my custom, I had asked Jess Ørnsbo who, in his opinion, might be interested in this type of theatre. He gave me a few names, one of which was Christian Ludvigsen. He had translated Ionesco and Beckett into Danish, and had been one of the founders of Fiolteatret, a small theatre which presented texts by 'experimental' authors, both Danish and foreign. That was how I came to know Christian Ludvigsen and his wife Silvia, also a theatre scholar, who welcomed me into their home and played such an important part in my life[36].

To return to Poland, I needed a visa: a pure formality since I had a scholarship. It was therefore a shock when the Polish Consulate in Oslo refused to give me one, on the grounds that I was a *persona non grata*. No other explanation was given. I was at a loss. Completely stunned by this, I wrote to Grotowski telling him what had happened. Suddenly and unexpectedly, from one day to the next, my close daily association with Grotowski and his theatre was interrupted. Everything I owned remained in Opole: books, records, work notes, clothes.

There I was in Norway with a useless train ticket to Poland, with enough money for barely a few days, and with a suitcase half full of

---

[35] The title changes reflect the fluctuations in what, according to Grotowski and me, was the focal point of the Theatre's New Testament. First it was called *The Psycho-Dynamic Theatre*, as an indication of its devastating effect on the psyche of the spectator (emphasis was above all placed on the archetype and the dialectic of apotheosis and derision). Then it became *In Search of Lost Theatre*, an allusion to theatre as ritual, as a ceremony that involves a community and is a vital and essential part of its spiritual life.

[36] After my visit we remained in contact by letter. Christian taught at the Institute of Dramaturgy of the University of Århus where Tage Hind was a lecturer. He too was interested in Grotowski and, later on, in Odin Teatret. When I began to publish the magazine *Teatrets Teori og Teknikk* in Oslo in 1965, Christian reviewed it and in the November of the same year he organised a tour of Denmark with *Ornitofilene*, Odin Teatret's first production. When Odin Teatret moved to Holstebro, in Denmark, he went to great lengths to help us by contacting the Danish Ministry of Culture as well as many well-known authors. It was thanks to him that Ole Sarvig and Peter Seeberg wrote texts for our theatre. Christian was our literary adviser and a member of Odin Teatret's Board of Directors for more than twenty years.

booklets on theatre as collective self-penetration. It was late April 1964 and there was still snow in Oslo's streets. I was confused as I wandered through those streets, yet filled with the sweetness of return to the city I had left four years before and which I thought of as home.

Second Flashback

Many are the countries that I have admired, that have fascinated me, and where I could have lived. But only two of them have I loved, abandoning myself to that love as one does when possessed by a passion: Norway and Poland.

It was Knut Hamsun who determined my life. In 1954, at the age of seventeen, after studying at a military college in Naples, I had hitchhiked to Copenhagen, then Stockholm. I worked as dishwasher, collected old newspapers or helped as a farmhand. While on a farm outside Stockholm I read *Under the Autumn Stars*, a novel by Knut Hamsun about a vagabond called August. The descriptions of northern Norway filled me with unknown longings. Instead of returning to Italy to study at university, I set off for the north, to Kiruna in Lapland, to work in a coal mine. It was a short stay. The police discovered that I had no work permit and immediately escorted me to the frontier, leaving me on the other side in Norway. I was in Narvik, in the same region where Hamsun's vagabonds had wandered. I went south, hitching lifts, for another two thousand kilometres. It was the end of October and snow was falling. It was freezing cold on the lorries in my summer clothes. I arrived in Oslo on my eighteenth birthday.

I found work as an apprentice in a sheet metal workshop. We worked with every type of sheet metal, constructing ventilation ducts for large buildings or transforming huge sheets of zinc into gutters which we attached to the eaves of houses. In summer and winter alike we climbed up onto roofs to carry out repairs, or to sweep away the snow when a heavy snowfall threatened them with collapse. Eigil Winnje, the owner of the workshop, had participated in the Resistance against the Germans and had been interned in Sachsenhausen. He treated me as a son and he taught me, with indulgence and humour, to weld.

Fridtjov Lehne was ten years older than me. He too had been in the Resistance. By day he was a journalist with the communist daily newspaper *Friheten* which was unable to pay him a salary. He earned his living as a night watchman at an old people's home. I met him by chance and he took me to his home. Sonja, his wife, was expecting their first child. They took me in and adopted me, sharing with me whatever they had.

They became my family. Fridtjov showed me what it meant to believe in an idea and to be prepared to pay the cost.

After the day's work I used to go to the library to read books in Italian. Kalle Orstad, an artist who painted during the day and worked as librarian in the evenings, asked me if I would be interested in being a paid model for one of his friends. I accepted. I was saving up for a long trip hitchhiking around the Mediterranean. Then I would go back to Rome to study law.

Willi Middelfart was quite a well-known painter. He had lived in Paris in the twenties and told me about Salmon and Mac Orlan, about le Douanier Rousseau and Gertrude Stein, about Max Jacob and the models Marie Laurencin and Suzanne Valadon (Utrillo's mother) who had become famous artists. During the thirties he became involved in politics. There is a painting of his in the Oslo National Gallery which shows the police charging strikers. I knew of nothing better than acting as model for Willi. In his spacious atelier, whose walls were covered with books and pictures, I read while I posed, looked at photos and reproductions, asked questions. Willi explained, linked up facts and ideas, clarified situations. Just as Fridtjov influenced me with his dream of a just society, without exploitation, Willi passed on to me a pleasure in what is superfluous yet necessary: art. Thanks to him, in the name of Ramakrishna, I boarded the *Talabot*, the ship which took me to India.

Talabot, on the other hand, made me discover the down-to-earth philosophical principles of Marx and Heraclitus: class struggle and *enantiodromia*, the way of opposites. The ports were not like I had imagined them: it could even happen that black people stank and that Christians lived like saints. I experienced the generosity of sailors and their racism. There came a day when I was forced to define myself with regard to others: 'dago, dirty Italian'. Should I accept or reject being treated in this way? A couple of small scars remind me of my disagreements with the more excitable sailors.

To get from the cabins to our workplaces in the stern, we had to climb over some railway engines destined for India. One day a sailor slipped and broke his leg. The crew's representative asked the captain to build a wooden walkway to make the passage safer. 'Your companion was drunk', replied the captain, and refused. The entire crew stopped work and declared a strike. Within an hour the captain gave the order to build the walkway.

In 1957 I disembarked. I intended to return to Italy to study law. It was Fridtjov who suggested I enrol at Oslo University for a semester: 'Like that you will get to know another Norwegian milieu'. I passed the preliminary exams: philosophy, psychology, logic, linguistics and Latin. During the day I worked as a welder, and in the evening I followed the courses at the university. I fell in with a group made up of the sons and daughters of intellectuals who, in the thirties, had created the Marxist movement, *Mot Dag* (Towards the Day). The children of these intellectuals who had all had careers within the social-democratic welfare state, were asking themselves how they could rebel against their parents without becoming reactionaries. Having a string of favourable prerequisites on my side, I became quite popular with them: I was a worker and, in addition, a foreigner (of which there were not many in Oslo at the time), I was more left-wing than them and I had the habit of presenting girls with flowers.

This group, called Husbygrenda after the neighbourhood in which they lived, was active in the SOSTUD, Socialistisk Studentlag, the student organisation of the social-democratic party. I distinguished myself by my faith in art as an instrument in the evolution of the working classes. With the help of Willi Middelfart I succeeded in borrowing paintings by him and his friends, and I organised exhibitions in factory canteens. It was Fridtjov who put me in contact with the union representatives who were mostly communists.

After the preliminary exams, I continued with French literature, and then I spent four months travelling on foot and hitchhiking round Greece and Turkey with Ole Daniel Bruun, a young bricklayer who wanted to become an architect. I set about studying Norwegian literature, finishing in 1959. But I needed a third subject to obtain my degree. By now I had difficulty in taking seriously my original plan that 'next year I shall return to Italy and become a lawyer'.

During all these years spent in Norway, I had often been faced with a dilemma: how should I behave? As an Italian so that I stood out from the others, or should I put a Nordic patina on my Mediterranean way of acting and thinking? For example, I had devised a complicated scenario when I was attracted to a girl. To impress her, I did not invite her out dancing or to the cinema, but to the theatre. I bought seats in the gallery but, as the theatres were half empty, we sat in the first row of the stalls. This made a great impression, and after the show the girl invited me to supper in return. But the performances were terribly boring. I could not understand why, no matter what the actors did, or how they reacted or spoke their lines, they were always so predictable.

I had already tried writing short stories, but in what language? Norwegian? Italian? Inspired by Willi, I had started to paint. But my illusions of becoming a painter soon vanished. I tried becoming a pianist and went to lessons once a week, but my welder's fingers were as rigid as chopsticks. I bought a trumpet to give vent to my artistic aspirations (the trumpet which I later sold to meet my debts in Poland). On going to the theatre, I discovered that there existed a profession – theatre direction – in which you sat in a chair with a cigarette between your fingers, giving everyone orders, and you were considered an artist. It was the solution to my problems of identity as an immigrant. I could be different and do whatever I wanted, and everybody would say that I was 'original'. I decided to study directing. But where? There were no schools for directors in Norway.

Then I saw *Ashes and Diamonds*, the film by Andrzej Wajda. As an Italian I could not ask the Norwegian state for a scholarship to study in Poland, and I had been away from Italy for six years. I asked my mother in Rome to approach the Foreign Ministry and she found out that there were specialist scholarships available for university post-graduates. I was not one, but I sent the certificates for my exams, written in Norwegian, as proof of my degree, and applied for a scholarship. I packed my bags, including the trumpet that I wanted to learn to play at the Chopin Conservatoire in Warsaw, and left for Israel to spend a couple of weeks in the sun. I waited more than six months, but in the end I received confirmation: the scholarship was mine. At the beginning of January 1961 I arrived in Poland, the promised land, the land of ashes and diamonds.

Hungering for Theatre

In April 1964, after being thrown out of Poland, I was back in Oslo, Knut Hamsun's Cristiania, whose streets he had roamed, dying of hunger and intent on becoming a writer. I had no money, but I took the decision to reduce working to earn money to a minimum. Every minute had to be devoted to becoming a director. I experienced daily the generosity of my friends. Sonja and Fridtjov Lehne, the communist family who had adopted me in 1954; Guri and Ole Daniel Bruun, the bricklayer who had become an architect; Erling Lægreid, a university friend and budding journalist; the painter Willi Middelfart; Knut Kristiansen, lecturer in Sanskrit at the university; the writer Jens Bjørneboe and his wife, Tone, who was an actress – they all helped me, accepting my obsession without question. The situation improved when I married Judy, the English girl I had met during those crucial days of the ITI Congress in Warsaw, and with whom I had gone to India. She supported the family by working as a secretary.

In order to be taken into consideration I had to possess certificates.

I resolved to finish university since I only needed to pass a few more exams. In the beginning my choice fell on Sanskrit and Indian philosophy, the *samkhya* system. A year and a half later, however, I took my degree in history of religion with a thesis on Sufism.

I went round all the theatres in Oslo offering myself as a director. But I had no diploma and Grotowski's name was totally unknown. I contacted actors who I knew were dissatisfied with their conditions of work: young and old, men and women, proposing that we might together create an experimental theatre. They were friendly but sceptical. I had read that many of our century's reformers had worked with amateurs: Stanislavsky, Meyerhold, Brecht, García Lorca. It was amazing how many amateur groups existed in Oslo, but none was prepared to abandon the gratification and pleasure of the amateur for the discipline of the 'psycho-dynamic' theatre that I was suggesting.

What did I really need? First of all, actors. But 'real' actors were not interested in working with me. So I would have to search for people in the same circumstances as myself: hungering for theatre and yet unable to satiate this hunger. There were a hundred or so of these individuals in Oslo: young people who had been rejected by the national theatre school. I obtained their addresses, invited them to a meeting and kindled in them the idea of becoming the chosen ones who would bring about an artistic revolution. On October 1st 1964 we created Odin Teatret.

I also wanted to publish a magazine which contained the *essential* texts for an actor or director, of the type that I wish I had been able to find myself, thereby avoiding the frustrations and the hours wasted on mediocre reading. I managed to convince Tore Giljane, editor of *Bonytt*, a magazine on architecture and interior design, to add a supplement on theatre. Hence the birth of *TTT*, *Teatrets Teori og Teknikk*. That was in October 1965. Two thirds of the first issue were devoted to Grotowski.

In February of the same year *In Search of Lost Theatre* was published in Italy. I had begun writing it in 1962 when Ferenc Hont, director of the Centre of Theatre Studies in Budapest, had visited Grotowski in Opole and was keen to diffuse his theories. He had said, with a smile: 'Clearly what you are doing is formalism and your theories are ideologically blame-worthy. We could print them in a special limited series about reprehensible theatre practices'. Hungary too was under a communist regime, but suffered no shortage of sharp brains. So it was that I started to jot down in French the description of everything I knew and had seen in Opole, and in April 1963 I posted the typed manuscript entitled *The Psycho-Dynamic Theatre* to Budapest. I was continually typing extra copies for people who came to visit us or for those abroad who wanted more detailed information in order to write about Grotowski's theatre.

Giampiero Bozzolato was a professor of Italian at Cracow University. We were on friendly terms and met each time I visited his town. He came to see me in Opole and read my psycho-dynamic *opus*. He directed the series *Sarmatica* with the publishers Marsilio in Padua and was prepared to publish my book if I translated it from French into Italian. We made an agreement that with my royalties Marsilio would invite Grotowski to Italy and arrange lectures for him. It would be killing three birds with one stone: the publication of a book on Grotowski; the Polish authorities would have to recognise that he was known abroad and give him a passport for the lectures; thus he would be able to promote his ideas in person.

Bozzolato asked me to change the title. *The Psycho-Dynamic Theatre* would not have sold many copies. I decided on *In Search of Lost Theatre* which, apart from its Proustian connotation, evoked the vision that guided Grotowski at that time: theatre as a 'secular' ritual.

After many tribulations the Italian version appeared at the same time as the 'reprehensible' Hungarian one. Grotowski, together with Ryszard Cieślak, was invited to Italy by Marsilio in May 1965 and gave lectures in Padua, Milan and Rome. His visit, which was badly organised, was not a success. His name was virtually unknown and there was no Raymonde Temkine to establish contacts, give him advice and create waves in artistic circles.

In the meantime Odin Teatret[37], which was working in conditions of total obscurity, felt that it was time to bring Grotowski's Teatr-Laboratorium to Oslo. We established a collaboration with Fylkingen, a Swedish cultural organisation, and with Copenhagen University's student theatre. The Norwegian Ministry of Foreign Affairs gave a small grant. My Norwegian friends guaranteed the rest of the money.

An almost insurmountable problem was finding the right venue. Grotowski's performance needed a large empty room with a wooden floor and with the possibility of providing total darkness. It was impossible to make people understand that this was for a theatre performance. In those days, when one spoke of theatre everyone thought of a stage and an auditorium. In the end we rented the meeting room of the Norwegian industrialists' association which was luxuriously spacious and had a parquet floor worthy of the 'poor theatre'. The members of the Teatr-

---

[37] Odin Teatret then consisted of four actors, all under the age of twenty: Anne Trine Grimnes, Else Marie Laukvik, Tor Sannum and Torgeir Wethal.

Laboratorium were housed at the homes of the Odin actors or with friends.

In February 1966 the Teatr-Laboratorium crossed the Polish border for the first time and took one of its productions abroad.

There are moments of happiness so intense that one is afraid. I was not afraid but stunned by *The Constant Prince*. No performance had ever had such an effect on me, making me fly, only to return to earth again as a changed person. My foundations were turned upside down, and I was unable to understand what had happened to those actors who I knew so well. In the productions by the 13 Rzędów that I had seen, Ryszard Cieślak was a secondary actor. The protagonists had always been the brilliant Zygmunt Molik (*Dziady, Kordian, Akropolis, Studium o Hamlecie*) and Zbigniew Cynkutis (*Kordian, Doctor Faustus*). Now I was watching Cieślak in the role of the protagonist: a spirit and at the same time a lion dancing on the point of a pin. It was a vision that left a mark on my soul. Even today, my dream as a director is that each one of my actors should take possession of each of his or her spectators just as Ryszard Cieślak did with me. Ryszard and I never really became friends, but his Constant Prince accompanies me and will stay beside me to the end.

The disconcerted Norwegian press formulated the objections that were to accompany and sustain the Grotowskian 'legend' from then on. Could his technique be applied to a contemporary text? Why so few spectators? Why so much mysticism? It was like a sweetened paraphrase of the Polish reviews. Four months later, in June, the Teatr-Laboratorium participated in the Théâtre des Nations directed by Jean-Louis Barrault. Once again Paris fulfilled its role as a sounding board; in the space of ten days, amid perplexity, stupor, rejection and enthusiasm, the extraordinary qualities of Grotowski, his actors and those collaborating with the ensemble which he had succeeded in creating, were recognised.

Holstebro

In June 1966 Odin Teatret left Oslo and, with the exception of one actor, moved to Holstebro in Denmark, a town of 18,000 inhabitants in the sparsely populated Northwest Jutland. The municipality had given us an empty farm on the outskirts of the town and a grant corresponding to about fifteen thousand dollars a year. In exchange we had promised to start a 'theatre laboratory'.

Barely a month later, in July, we organised our first activity, a two-week seminar with Grotowski, Ryszard Cieślak and Stanisław Brzozowski who was the main actor in Henryk Tomaszewski's mime theatre in Wrocław.

There were thirty participants from all over Scandinavia. I was astonished, and also embarrassed, to see well-known artists from the Royal Theatre in Copenhagen and other theatre companies throw themselves into essentially 'physical' exercises. Such an approach was quite new at the time – not just the training, the physical and vocal exercises which did not stem from the interpretation of a text, but also the very idea of organising a seminar, not as a round table or a debate but as a practical situation that dealt with the work of the actors on themselves.

Thus we inaugurated a tradition which lasted until half way through the seventies. Odin Teatret organised two seminars every year, one in the spring lasting a week, around a specific theme (commedia dell'arte, the scenic language, the author and group theatre, Indonesian theatre, Japanese theatre, etc.); the other, of two to three weeks in July, on 'training'. In 1966, 1967, 1968 and 1969 Grotowski participated together with other artists. In 1966 we from Odin Teatret also took part in the teaching. The following years we devoted ourselves exclusively to the organisation. For us, the seminars were an opportunity to get to know the work of artists who interested us and, at the same time, to earn money. All the practical work was carried out by Odin people: administration, translation, cleaning, preparing meals, washing up, transportation. In this way costs were kept to a minimum, and with the grants and subscription fees we could pay the artists and also put a little money on one side. In addition we were promoting an activity that no other institution carried out at the time in Denmark, thereby justifying our designation of 'laboratory'.

The seminars were also opportunities to reunite friends and sympathisers. Eric Veaux came, and Marc Fumaroli, a specialist of rhetoric and the baroque, future Professor at the Collège de France and member of the Académie Française. The Danish poet Ole Sarvig came, and so did designer Jakob Jensen, not to mention Norwegian, Swedish and Polish friends. The participants lived free of charge in private homes, on the invitation of local families, or else at an agricultural college in rooms with two or more beds. For the seminar we used the gym and classrooms in a primary school which the municipality had placed at our disposal. Grotowski usually lived in a tiny flat which Else Marie Laukvik, one of the Odin actresses, lent him. He always told her that it was full of spiders that bit him while he slept, filling her with feelings of guilt. We used to meet there at night to talk, or else we would go out somewhere in town. One night we went to the agricultural school where Fumaroli was staying and woke him up by whispering 'police' in his ear. He woke with a start, only to be met with uproarious laughter from Grotowski and me. It ended with all three of us drinking in the room with the invisible spiders.

In 1967 the seminar lasted three weeks. Together with Grotowski, Cieślak and Brzozowski, we also invited Charles Marowitz, the American director who had collaborated with Peter Brook in the Royal Shakespeare Company's Theatre of Cruelty season in 1963. There was also Renée Saurel, the French critic and Ellen Stewart, La Mama, who presented a production.

That year I had thought of bringing together the various theatre 'methods' which had grown up in the communist countries, and had invited Helene Weigel, Barbara Schall, Ekkehard Schall (Brecht's wife, daughter and son-in-law respectively), Joachim Tenschert (*dramaturg*) and Manfred Wekwerth (director) of the Berliner Ensemble. Agnete Strøm, our administrator, and Judy went to East Berlin to speak to Helene Weigel who was apparently keen to return to Denmark, a country in which she had lived in exile for five years, and which she remembered with pleasure after nearly twenty years' absence. We had made contact in Denmark with Fredrik Martner, a social-democratic journalist who had been a friend of Brecht's in the thirties, had written a book about him and had remained on excellent terms with his family. Martner had written to Helene Weigel in Berlin and had given us a letter of presentation. We were thrilled at the idea of having the best names of the Brecht tradition at the same time as Grotowski and Cieślak.

In the beginning everything went well. Then silence. There was no reply to our letters, registered letters and telegrams. We telephoned, but Helene Weigel was always busy. Finally Martner led us to understand that they would not be coming. Helene Weigel had discovered that Odin Teatret was not a famous institution and, to make things worse, was in the provinces. It would have been beneath their dignity for the Berliner Ensemble to participate. Martner commented: 'That is the way of thinking that has saved Brecht. Learn from it!' We learnt, but we were unable to make the Berliner Ensemble meet the Teatr-Laboratorium.

In 1968, our spirits in no way dampened by what happened the previous year, we considered a meeting between Ingmar Bergman and Grotowski. Bergman replied immediately with a very short but polite letter: he was busy. Later I found out that he did not appreciate Grotowski[38].

That year, apart from the veterans Grotowski, Cieślak and Brzozowski, Jolanda Rodio, an opera singer and voice teacher, was present, as were Carlo,

---

[38] However, Donya Feuer, an American choreographer who later collaborated closely with Bergman, both in theatre and cinema, did participate in our seminar.

Alfredo and Romano Colombaioni, the clowns and actors who had participated together with Dario Fo and Franca Rame in our spring seminar.

The Holstebro seminars were, at the time, amongst the longest of those
directed by Grotowski. As usual there were thirty participants, most of
whom that year were American. They transformed the place into a corner
of America and every day exulted over the feats of the first (American)
astronaut on the moon, and complained about Grotowski's intransigence.
Sometimes there were violent clashes in which Grotowski remained
imperturbable while I attempted to pick up the pieces.

In 1969 Grotowski came without Cieślak[39]. He observed and
commented on the performances and the training of the participants,
many of whom came as complete theatre groups.

Right from the start Grotowski preferred working in the evening or at
night. Since the 1966 seminar, the participants trained with the other
guest artists during the morning and afternoon. From the late afternoon
on, it was the turn of Cieślak and Grotowski who entered the work room
without watches and with no idea when they would finish. Sometimes
they even continued late after the evening meal, and this could be
disagreeable and also irritating for the other artists, and for the participants who started early the following morning. The doors were locked
and no one could enter once they had begun. Grotowski spoke French.
The first year, I translated for him. The following years Ulf Ekeram, a
Swedish pedagogue and director, took over. Grotowski's comments, reflections and speeches could last for hours. The taking of notes was not
allowed. People were exhausted. Some lay down and fell asleep, to the
obvious irritation of Grotowski.

He came over as the essence of intolerance: a figure clothed in black
from head to foot, his eyes hidden behind sunglasses, seated at a table,
sometimes raised up on the stage. If someone refuted one of his assertions
(and it could happen, with the presence of established actors from the
traditional theatre or with the critics), he would react strongly,
overwhelming his hapless victim. As organiser all complaints and dissen-
sions fell on me. It happened that the odd person left the seminar
shouting at me that the time of concentration camps was over. Others
furiously attacked Odin Teatret for, contrary to the democratic Danish
tradition, passively accepting Grotowski's dictatorial caprices. He,
meanwhile, lived separate from the others, did not mix with the other

---

[39] Also invited were Joe Chaikin, the actor/director and founder of the Open Theater, and
once again Jolanda Rodio.

artists, and turned up fresh in the afternoon, ready to give his utmost. I did my best to emulate him, and I refused admission to a young French director, Arianne Mnouchkine, who arrived in Holstebro when the seminar had already begun.

In 1966, as well as commenting on and intervening in training sessions conducted by Ryszard Cieślak who taught physical and plastic exercises, Grotowski led an improvisation involving all the participants. The protagonists were Torgeir Wethal, Odin Teatret's actor, and Martha Westin, a director and actress from a Swedish group. The theme was a wedding party and we were all the guests. Seated around tables, we had to improvise a song in low voices while Torgeir and Martha followed directions whispered to them by Grotowski. At a certain point we were told to lean our heads on the table and *not to look*, while continuing to hum. For a long time Grotowski worked with Martha and Torgeir. Finally, when we emerged from that solitary yet collective universe, we saw the faces of Torgeir and Martha shining as though touched by Grace.

Sometimes Grotowski worked with only one participant in the presence of everybody. For more than an hour we witnessed how he stimulated the actor with images, opening up the entire range of resonators and the regions of a secret and most profound voice. They were quite exceptional moments and the most moving thing of all was Grotowski's sense of delicacy and protection towards the actors who entrusted themselves totally to him. It was in blatant contrast to his behaviour when speaking *ex cathedra*.

Cieślak, who led the training, had the capacity to surprise us every year, changing everything that he had taught at the previous seminar. One year every exercise had to be rooted in personal images or motivations, following a calm, almost dreamlike rhythm. The following year, the exercises had to be carried out in relation to those of the other participants who were training simultaneously in the same space, in a playful attitude, like a succession of encounters and flights towards other stimuli. The final year, you had to go beyond your own limits and burst into a controlled whirlwind of forces and tensions. At times, those participants who did not give up radiated a special quality of energy; at others, there was only tiredness and even occasional accidents[40].

---

[40] Descriptions exist of these work sessions. One of the most detailed and fascinating is to be found in Marianne Ahrne's novel, *Katarina Horowitz drömmar* (The Dreams of Katarina Horowitz), Nordstedts Forlag, Stockholm, 1990, which has page after page dealing with this experience, concentrating on the subjective consequences, on a profoundly personal level, of the exercises and improvisations led by Cieślak and Grotowski.

Cieślak was indefatigable, urging the participants to surpass their own limits, to overstep the bounds of their own possibilities, spurring them on even when they were exhausted. He set an example by devoting himself to the utmost to each individual participant. He performed each exercise with an unimaginable range of variations, of rhythmic nuances, and with an indescribable quality of vigour and vulnerability. More and more often, however, the expressive characteristics of the 'constant prince' came to the surface. I have often asked myself if he was imprisoned by that role or whether, on the contrary, it made him discover his innermost identity which was now present in all his actions.

After the 1969 seminar, it became clear that Grotowski would not be doing any more of them. He had come alone, as though the possibilities of renewal in Cieślak's training had suddenly been exhausted. Grotowski himself, in '69, was not a stimulative element but rather a reactive one, observing and commenting. Three years had passed since the Paris success and his name aroused expectations all over the world. Only in Poland had the situation remained unchanged. Grotowski had to take into account the political games of the regime, and he depended on official invitations to travel abroad. I had some money which I gave him so that he could visit India. He left Holstebro in the direction of the land of Maharishi, where he stayed for a month[41].

Towards A Poor Theatre

The first issue of *Teatrets Teori og Teknikk* - abbreviated to *TTT* - in October 1965 was for the most part devoted to Grotowski, and for the rest to Jacques Poliéri, the French scenographer and avant-garde director who was the inventor, in 1960, of the 'annular mobile theatre' in which the performance surrounded the spectators. Odin Teatret published 23 issues of the magazine, up until May 1975, alternating between 'classics' like Piscator's *The Political Theatre*, Zeami's *The Secret Tradition of Noh Theatre*, Meyerhold's *The Theatrical Theatre* and Eisenstein's *Notes on Direction*. Texts by or on Grotowski were published in No. 8 and No. 20 while two other issues, Nos. 7 and 18, were devoted entirely to him. No. 18 included

---

[41] The Holstebro seminars left lasting impressions in the memories and experience of those who participated in them. For some, the consequences were unforeseeable, even extreme. In Odin's archives we still have shorthand texts of Grotowski's speeches which the budding Swedish film director and writer, Marianne Ahrne, patiently noted down at the end of the seminars from an old tape recorder which, unknown to Grotowski, had been hidden in the work room. After the first seminar I told Grotowski about my subterfuge and he approved it. From then on he corrected the transcriptions and occasionally turned them into 'canonical' texts.

his articles *Physical Exercises, Vocal Exercises* and *Not Actor, but Son of Man*; also *Grotowski and the Indian Tradition* by Maria Krzysztof Byrski, a long open letter to Grotowski from Eric Bentley, and an interview with Ryszard Cieślak. No. 7 constituted an event beyond limited Scandinavian circles and was published, not as a magazine in Danish, but as a book in English. Its title was: *Towards a Poor Theatre*.

In 1968, I had thought again of devoting a whole *TTT* to Grotowski on the occasion of the annual summer seminar at Odin Teatret at which he was one of the teachers. It was to comprise three long interviews from 1967, and all the articles that he had written so far, four in all, Flaszen's texts on *Akropolis* and *The Constant Prince*, as well as several chapters from my *In Search of Lost Theatre*. Grotowski, who was particularly interested in recording the development of the training, proposed an account by the director, Frans Marijnen of a seminar he had held in Brussels.

I had the idea of publishing the magazine in English in order to sell it to the foreign participants of the seminar. It would not cost more since Judy was English and had worked as a translator at the ITI. I considered publishing all these heterogeneous texts as a book instead of in the customary format of the magazine. I had not yet thought of a title.

It became an arduous and complicated project. Grotowski began re-elaborating his texts which had already been translated, making additions and cuts. Marijnen's text only existed in Flemish, so I had to find someone to collaborate with Judy for the English translation. Most time was wasted in the final revision of each text. Grotowski meticulously checked every single word. Although at that point he did not speak English, he insisted on preserving the construction of certain French phrases (a language in which he was now able to read and express himself), even though in English they acquired a different meaning or were quite simply meaning-less. Judy, who was pregnant, was irritated and exhausted, but equally obstinate in defending the syntax and correctness of her language. I attempted to mediate. I was familiar with Grotowski's linguistic uncon-ventionality and his obsessive punctiliousness over translation, but I was also aware of how the value of the book could be diminished by a forced and clumsy English style. This may seem like a perfectly obvious fact, but in practice it was a struggle. We could spend a whole evening deciding how to translate a single sentence.

It was clear that there had been a shift in Grotowski's priorities. In Opole, his thoughts were concentrated on the construction of the performance as a 'secular' ritual and the psychic and emotional conse-quences it must have on the spectator. He used the archetype as a common substratum and point of encounter between actors and spectators, and the dialectic of apotheosis and derision as a tool to revive a common nucleus of experiences. He spoke of 'theatre magic', of the actorshaman, capable of extraordinary feats. The supremacy of the actor was accentuated by the introduction of the training.

After my departure from Opole, and after the move to Wrocław and the work on *The Constant Prince* with Ryszard Cieślak, something changed. Now the central concern had become the actor's 'total act' and the process by which it was achieved. Even for Grotowski the results attained by Cieślak in *The Constant Prince* must have been a surprise and perhaps a shock; so much so as to bring explicitly to the forefront that which had always been of fundamental interest to him: 'technique 2', the moment of individual transcendence which occurred through 'technique 1', the actor's craft.

Now Grotowski spoke less of archetypes and the dialectic of apotheosis and derision, and more of 'poor theatre' and *via negativa*. This definition had to appear in the title of the book. What is more, it had to be stressed that it was not a question of an aesthetic, a technique, a system, but of something that was open, in motion: a process. What about calling it 'The Poor Theatre'[42]? No, that was too static. It sounded like a manifesto. It was the preposition 'towards' that was our salvation, immediately evoking associations with Craig's book, *Towards a New Theatre*. In addition it recalled the Polish title of Grotowski's article published in *Odra: Ku teatrowi ubogiemu*[43]. So it was that an issue of a Danish magazine first became an anthology in English of texts by various authors and ended up as *Towards a Poor Theatre* by Jerzy Grotowski.

My editorial experience was limited to that of *TTT* which was never printed in more than a thousand copies. Such was my faith in the success of the book - the first from my master and furthermore in an international language - that I decided to print five thousand copies. Tadeusz Jackowski, the Polish graphic artist who had helped me in Poland, designed the cover: the Sea of Tranquillity on the moon or a desert panorama with the different depths and shades of colour of Siena's earth. Looking at it, I dreamed of the imaginary Himalayas of the soul, and of blood stains on a wall that have been dried by time and transformed into moss. A dust jacket of glossy paper took up the graphic symbol of *The Constant Prince* and its motto: 'Because Earth is the abode of our bound-

---

[42] This was the title of the article published in *TDR - Tulane Drama Review* in the spring of 1976.
[43] See letters 18 and 19 from Grotowski of 5 September and 27 September 1965.

less voyage'. The book was to be ready in June. The seminar to be held by Grotowski and Cieślak would begin in July.

When the lorry arrived and began to unload package after package of copies of *Towards a Poor Theatre*, the joy of holding the first book from the Odin Teatret publishing house was buried under an avalanche of five thousand volumes. Every spare space, every corner of our theatre was invaded by piles of books. Two more shocks were to follow: the bill to be paid which was far in excess of the estimated cost,[44] and the depressing realisation that nobody was buying the book. No enthusiastic reactions had welcomed its publication. To dream of world distribution by our theatre was sheer folly.

Our literary adviser, Christian Ludvigsen, introduced me to Martin Berg, a writer who also owned a small publishing house for avant-garde writers and children's books. Martin agreed to become our agent, wrote to his contacts abroad and presented the book at international book fairs. He also did all he could to resolve the critical situation that Odin Teatret found itself in because we were unable to pay the printer's bill. This insolvency threatened the survival of the theatre. After long negotiations, Martin managed to persuade the printer to let us pay in three instalments[45].

A year passed before we began to sell the translation rights in other countries: in France thanks to the indefatigable Raymonde Temkine, and in Italy through Ferruccio Marotti who became interested in Odin Teatret after seeing *Ferai* at the Venice Biennale. I remember those first months after the publication. Foreign friends who came to visit us in Holstebro put five or ten copies in their suitcases which they then sold in their own countries, sending the money to us. More than twenty years were to go by before the Odin had sold all of its five thousand English copies.

No other book on theatre this century has had the sudden impact of *Towards a Poor Theatre*. Craig's *On the Art of the Theatre*, in 1905, was linked in its absolute originality to a theatre revolution whose breeding grounds were already established, scattered across Europe, and including Stanislavsky and Meyerhold. But Grotowski's book appeared at a particular moment and had characteristics which set it apart from other 'foundational books' of our century.

---

[44] Grotowski and I were unaware then that corrections to the proofs were an expensive affair. There were also many more photos than originally planned.

[45] This difficult situation marked the start of a close friendship with Martin Berg who became an invaluable collaborator and member of Odin Teatret's Board of Directors for more than 25 years.

The Euro-American theatre was shaken by new needs. The first to express these were the playwrights Ionesco, Beckett, Adamov, Mrożek, Arrabal and Weiss who had introduced themes and new ways of telling stories on stage, forcing a form of acting that was different to the verisimilitude of mainstream theatre.

May 1968 was barely over and there was a need for commitment, renewal and a desire to rediscover in the theatre the political, ethical and social meaning that had characterised the research of the theatre reformers of the first three decades of the twentieth century.

Grotowski's book appeared when the legend of his productions was widespread. Only a very few people had actually seen *Akropolis* and *The Constant Prince*. Everything that was written about his theatre, the way it was described, the prejudices, the misunderstandings, the gossip, the anecdotes, the enthusiasm, the fantasies surrounding his productions and the training of the actors, all this created the legend and was decisive.

Towards a Poor Theatre confronts the principal problems facing an actor or a director. It begins with the first step – the technical preparation – with page upon page describing exercises. It opens up radical dramaturgical perspectives, until then unthinkable, about ways of approaching the texts which tradition has handed down to us. It presents the vision of a theatre, which goes beyond its characteristics of artistic performance or entertainment, reaffirming its simultaneously sacred and secular vocation of collective ritual. There is an uncompromising rejection of the 'old' theatre exemplified in the comparison between the 'actor courtesan' and the 'holy actor'. The difference between these two is the same as that between the ability of a courtesan and the disposition of true love to give and receive: in other words, self-sacrifice. It is a vision which on the one hand gives back to the actor and the director the possibility of total commitment, and on the other allows them to rediscover a freedom beyond the circle of merchants, ideologists and fashions. Never before had a book been written in which there was room for both the great obsessions as well as the concrete aspects of the craft. It was truly the Theatre's New Testament. Each sentence spoke to each one of its readers in a different language: intimate, technical, dramaturgical, social, esoteric, political, moral. But always a language of fire.

I could describe the tortuous paths followed by this book before falling into the hands of a Peruvian, a Belgian, an Australian or a Japanese; how it had turned their lives upside down and led them to break with a theatre practice which appeared to be their only destiny. But I was unaware of all this during those months in 1968 in my small provincial town while I read in the newspapers about student revolt, and was struggling with my publishing problems.

And yet I discovered in the history of those days a concrete example of Grotowski's vision. It was embodied in Jan Palach, the student of theatre studies, who had set fire to himself in Prague in 1968 as a protest against the Russian invasion of his country. Incarnated in the solitary gesture of this twenty-year-old youth I saw the archetype; I recalled Kordian, Prometheus, Winkelried, Christ, the individual who, by assuming responsibility for others, truly accomplishes that act of self-sacrifice which is demanded of the actor. And while I tried to find the money to pay the bill for the book of my elder brother, and Martin Berg and Christian Ludvigsen did their best to defend me from the printer's lawyers, I reflected on Jan Palach, my younger brother. And both brothers accompanied me during rehearsals of *Ferai*.

The Last Production

The premiere of *Apocalypsis cum figuris*, Grotowski's last production, took place in February 1969. The preparation process had lasted nearly four years. It had begun in the autumn of 1965 with *Samuel Zborowski*, by Słowacki. Then, in the course of 1966, it had concentrated on the Gospel, ending up with a montage of texts from the Bible, T.S. Eliot, Dostoevsky and Simone Weil.

Together with Grotowski, we set up a three-week programme at Odin Teatret with performances, meetings and television interviews. In mid-August 1971 Grotowski arrived with all his actors, Ludwik Flaszen, Zbigniew Osiński and a couple of official representatives from Wrocław and from PAGART, the Polish government agency that served as intermediary for every theatre ensemble that went abroad. After London and New York, it was the third time that *Apocalypsis cum figuris* left Poland. We presented twelve performances, organising an "airlift" for spectators coming from Copenhagen.

Odin Teatret interrupted rehearsals of *Min Fars Hus* (My Father's House) and concentrated on their reception. Alluding to the international success of *Ferai*, our previous production, but also to himself and the new production that he was taking on tour, Grotowski teased me with the story of Bilbolbu, a director from deepest Africa who had been invited with his theatre to Paris. He is an instant success, acclaimed by everybody and the critics declare him a genius. A year later, Bilbulba, another director from even deeper Africa, arrives in Paris with his company. The public is enthusiastic, the critics are ecstatic; there are interviews and awards. When leaving his hotel, triumphant and happy, Bilbulba sees a beggar who asks him for money: 'Give me a franc, I too was famous last year – the beggar whispers to him – I am Bilbolbu.'

Apocalypsis cum figuris was presented in two versions: one for about forty spectators seated on benches, and the other for an audience of about a hundred, standing or else seated on the floor. This last version was only for young people and there were four of these performances in Holstebro. Grotowski and I spoke together at length about this: a performance restricted to young people seemed to me to be discrimination and yielding to the cult of youth which was gaining ground in the Euro-American civilisation. He maintained that it was uncomfortable for people who were no longer young to watch the performance standing or sitting on the floor. I insisted it was not right to put tickets on sale, then ask the buyers their ages, and finally refuse to sell if they were over thirty. The solution was to advertise only the 'seated' performances, organising the sale of tickets through written applications which included a brief *curriculum vitae*, and selecting the young people from amongst these.

One of the people who came from Copenhagen to see *Apocalypsis cum figuris* was Janka Katz, the Jewish poet from Cracow who was the first to mention the name of Grotowski to me and direct me to Opole. She had sought refuge in Denmark following the wave of anti-semitism that had swept across Poland in 1968. After the performance she asked to meet her old friend. With an almost imperceptible nod of the head Grotowski indicated the member of PAGART who followed him everywhere. I explained to Janka that it was not wise for a Pole to be seen speaking to someone who had 'chosen freedom' abroad. Janka was extremely upset and from then on we had no contact with each other.

At Odin Teatret we had a room that was completely black, including the floor and ceiling, where *Kaspariana* and *Ferai* had come into being. *Apocalypsis cum figuris* required a white ceiling which reflected the light from the spotlights pointed upwards, and a natural coloured wooden floor. We altered the appearance of our black room and so it has remained until today, twenty-five years later. I wanted to keep it like that to remind me of the visit by the theatre that was my origin.

Grotowski announced that he would not create any more productions, but he continued with an activity to which he gave various names. Over the next few years he spoke to me of this, describing the Polish political context, the impact on the young generation, his new collaborators, the difficulties and undertakings of the actors I knew from Opole. The core of his most intimate tensions and of his discourse was identical to that underlying our conversations in Opole. Then the terminology was theatrical, now it had changed, but I did not find it strange. The essence was the same as in the old days.

I, on the other hand, was venturing ever deeper into the theatre, into regions without theatre, 'bartering' theatre, wasting it in tumultuous and solitary parades. Odin Teatret's journeys in Europe and Latin America brought us in contact with our 'kin' who were submerged everywhere: the 'third theatre'. I asked myself, looking for an answer in action, how I could create a profoundly individualistic theatre, rooted in the most intimate necessity and representing a form of rejection of the surrounding norms of the time. Was it possible, through theatre, to follow the example of Renan's nihilist, Christ?

The Invisible Master

When Odin Teatret began, there were six of us: four actors, myself and Grotowski who, invisible, watched every detail of my work from a corner of the room. With him I could not cheat. When I was in doubt, I began walking backwards and forwards; in reality, I was approaching the corner to ask advice. I perceived, deep down inside myself, the indications he gave me and I put them into practice immediately, but camouflaging them in such a way that no one would recognise them. I did not want to be called an imitator. This was not merely personal vanity; I wanted people to say that his theatre and his ideas were capable of inspiring original results.

The master was always there, throughout the seventies, in that corner of the room towards which I was drawn. Not only did he help me to resolve problems and enigmas, but he also pointed out new fields of knowledge and awareness, like a Delphic oracle. It had become clear to me that the director's most difficult task consisted not in resolving problems, but in creating problems for himself, for the actors and for the spectators.

During those years the invisible master became even more important for me.

I realised that every new phase or development in the relationship between Grotowski and his actors preceded a similar situation in the Odin by two or three years. His 'paratheatrical' path displayed working relationships which were no longer based on the fusion of individualisms, in order to create a collective and structured performance. For me theatre remained an essentially solitary adventure which confirmed and at the same time denied itself through continual work with the same people, my actors. Grotowski's new interests had profoundly altered the bond with his actors, and other collaborators who were young and motivated by different needs had taken over from the older ones. Knowing about what was happening in Grotowski's group, discussing with him when we met, and reflecting on the professional and human consequences, helped me to identify similar potential temptations and symptoms in Odin Teatret.

Grotowski continuously confronted me with one inescapable fact: a theatre group, like any other organism grows old. The need for new relationships, new stimuli, new challenges drives the individual to seek out new paths in order to satisfy personal needs. This is what theatre history tells us since Copeau and Stanislavsky. Grotowski was pointing this tendency out to me, and I engaged in ceaseless discussions with my invisible master in the corner of the room. Must I too allow all this to happen to the Odin? Could I allow my companions of so many years and experiences that had been so important in my life, slip away, shaking off responsibility and rediscovering freedom, director only of my own life? Could I live my own 'adventure' now that I had a position, was accepted, and would be able to manage without the actors?

Throughout the seventies my conversations with the master increased. It was like when Grotowski and I drank cup after cup of tea at the station in Opole, with one of us speaking, raising questions, while the other remained silent like a mirror. The thousands of decisions, involving down to earth yet fundamental problems, that I took during those years were the result of this *corps à corps*, this wrestling with my invisible and incorporeal master.

It was a symbiosis of energies, thoughts, solutions and decisions with a partner whom I called Grotowski, but who was the Master. The Master advised me not to follow Grotowski but to go elsewhere. Or, better still, to remain elsewhere, together with my actors.

In 1982 I was returning from Cologne where I had been present at the editing of the film of *Come! And the Day Will be Ours*, one of Odin Teatret's productions. Suddenly the plane lost altitude in a startling fall that lasted for a second and seemed like an eternity. I found myself bathed in sweat and with one thought in my head: I am going to disappear. A couple of days later I gathered my actors together and announced that I was going away for three hundred and sixty-five days. I called it a sabbatical year.

It was a luminous period, of another kind of beauty to that which I experienced when I was with my actors. The pleasure of learning Japanese in Tokyo week after week, travelling like a penniless vagabond on the Trans-Siberian railway, on Osoresan or in India, the long march to the last village north of Quebec, and the endless hours of reading beside the stove in my house in the country, surrounded by my family.

Around that time Holstebro and Odin Teatret were places of refuge for Grotowski. He used to stay for long periods, especially after General Jaruzelski's *coup d'état* in 1981. He lived at the theatre, in a small room which our actress Else Marie Laukvik had tried to make more cosy with a white woollen rug. We exchanged impressions about the feeling of freedom which came from being a lone traveller and from devoting oneself to the Indies which are before our soul. Grotowski suffered over what was happening in Poland, over his colleagues who were at the mercy of circumstance, over his inability to do anything for them and over a fear that any decision he took might harm them.

When I returned to Odin Teatret in October 1983 I got down to preparing a production. I discovered that Grotowski was no longer in the corner of the room. I was alone with Iben Nagel Rasmussen and César Brie, the two actors with whom I was rehearsing.

I felt no sadness or apprehension, rather curiosity. Something had changed, and yet remained the same. I tried to decipher what it was that the master wanted to tell me through his disappearance. Who is this distant and invisible master? The professional superego? The person, or collection of people who have consciously or unconsciously led us to incorporate certain tensions that become the rudder for our most secret impulses, our most extreme decisions, our most punctilious achievements? Why does the master vanish? To let us know that from now on we are able to live without him, that we have become him or that what is essential is concealed *behind* his image?

I concentrated on work. I rediscovered the craftsman's pleasure in the finished detail, in the quality of the rhythm, the discovery of the melody in a sentence. However, I missed that presence in the corner of the room, that *Sunyata*, that emptiness filled by a voice which conversed with the blind horse within me.

Iben and César had asked me to work on a production about Nijinski and his wife Romola Pulszki. They brought me a photograph of the couple: amid trees in the courtyard of a house, a bald and corpulent man was supporting a middle aged-woman on tiptoe whose arms were raised above her head like a ballet dancer. A cruel and pathetic picture taken in Schloss Mittersill, in Austria, in 1946. That photograph was the seed which generated *Marriage with God, or The Impossible Love*.

I searched for texts to give a voice to the human adventure of Nijinski and Romula Pulszki. He had been called the god of dance and had suffered the ordeal of pain in body and mind; she had defended their love

and kept it alive. Once again I had the feeling that work on the performance consisted in breathing life into a sphinx which was confronting me
with an enigma: what point in your life have you reached?

I chose some texts:

Sometimes in the twilight, a face
peers at us from the depths of a mirror.
You are this mirror, cracking,
which reveals me my own face.

Each separation holds out a promise
of meeting again.

Don't run. Walk slowly.
Towards you alone you must go.
Walk slowly. Don't run.
For the child that is you,
eternal infant,
cannot follow.

If you wonder where you might find me
do not wander in mountains and forests
if you really want to find me
look for me in you, in your own heart.

The meeting between Jalal ad-Din Rumi, the respected ulema of Konya,
and Shams, a Sufi dervish, provided my main inspiration. Oblivious of
religious rituals and obligations, Rumi began to express his mystical
fervour by dancing and singing, amid the scandal of the orthodox
believers. Many of these rebuked Shams, accusing him of being responsible for Rumi's reprehensible, almost insane behaviour. Shams vanished.
Had he disappeared of his own will to help his disciple? Had he been
assassinated? Maddened by pain, Rumi shut himself in a room, whirling
as though he wanted to hide inside himself. He composed poems crying
out his desire for Shams who had led him on the path of Experience. And
then one day Rumi saw his Master again and recognised him. But it was
not Shams. It was the disciples who had been accompanying him for so
long in his solitude. Rumi returned to the light of the sun and allowed
himself to be guided by them.

When I finished *Marriage with God, or The Impossible Love*, I dedicated it to J. and S. Concealed behind these initials were Jerzy and Shams.

So the master is not there, silent and invisible, in a corner of the room. Like a Hindu divinity, he has numerous faces, eyes gazing in different directions, contrasting gestures, voices which deny one another: they are my actors, the people who for thirty-three, thirty, twenty-five, twenty years have accompanied me to the furthest limit beyond which you can only continue alone. And it is with gratitude and love that I encounter Grotowski who, from afar and unaware, has guided me every day towards my Master.

A Question Unanswered

Grotowski bursts out laughing when I tell him about the book I am writing and the reactions of certain friends and close collaborators who have read the manuscript.

It is May 1997 and we are in Pontedera. Grotowski is sixty-three years old and I have had my sixtieth birthday a few months ago. I tell him about the criticisms of these unfinished pages by my first readers. Their comments pointed out two dangers and one fundamental question, and for months these blocked my progress. The two dangers consisted in the excessive presence of my own person, and an unintentionally oversimplified interpretation of Grotowski's personality.

The necessity to tell the facts, as if chatting with old friends or young people, had led me to give a picaresque tone to my actions, making them stand out. My previewing readers had noticed that I always met extraordinary, fantastic, generous people. And they added: 'It is as though you wanted to insinuate that it was circumstances, chance or collaborators that had made Grotowski great.'

Thus the desire to shed light on the value of people who are forgotten today, ignored or scarcely mentioned in books about the historic adventure of the Teatr-Laboratorium 13 Rzędów had the opposite effect to the one intended. If I have told about Grotowski's human qualities as I knew him in the early sixties, when he was a long way from becoming a myth and never himself imagined that he would ever become one, it was because I wanted to bring back the atmosphere and circumstances of that period, and the courage of a nameless young man, solitary and awkward, who alone set himself up against the theatre of his whole country, against the fundamental principles of the profession, against the very way of conceiving culture and above all against a communist regime which curbed every attempt to escape from the norms it imposed.

It was not difficult to get around the two dangers. The real difficulty was to find an answer to the question that *all* the readers of the manuscript had asked in one form or another: 'What was the relationship between you and Grotowski? It's not at all clear from what you say. You never talk about it. You must have been extremely close. There is very little age difference between you, and yet he calls you Kim and you call him Lama. It may only be a joke, but it is obvious from his letters that he is very attached to you and concerned about you, and that you were a different person after the encounter with him. What happened? What was there between you that has kept this bond alive until today?' Some of my friends added, jokingly: 'Were you a homosexual couple?'.

At this point in my story Grotowski bursts out laughing, remarking what a pity it was that it had never occurred to us before because we could have had some fun out of it. Then we become serious again. I ask him how he would define our relationship during those years. It is this question which has become an obstacle. I understood that without finding an answer to it, what I had written was not complete. But I had no answer.

Grotowski reflects, his eyes half closed. He is very tired and ill. This morning he has come to the Town Hall of Pontedera because they are making me an honorary citizen of the town. The same recognition was bestowed on him a few years ago. The mayor has said that these honorary citizens are to constitute a group of 'wise senators' around the administrators of the town in Tuscany where Roberto Bacci's theatre centre has its base. So Grotowski and I joked about the fact that we are now fellow-citizens and have a country at last. He is exhausted, and his movements are even slower than usual. I wonder how he will be able to leave for Paris in a few days time. He has to give a lecture at the Collège de France where he has been appointed Professor of Theatre Anthropology.

The result of his reflection appears to be more a general consideration of our times than a real answer: in our culture, a relationship like that which existed between us in Poland is totally incomprehensible. It would have been far less so in certain Asian cultures or in another era.

I point out that it is not much of an answer for anyone who obviously wishes to understand and accuses me of being evasive. What is his opinion on how our relationship came about, and why has it lasted in spite of the years and the different roads we have taken?

Grotowski speaks at length about our characters which are complementary, not only in practical, visible terms: I, the extrovert; he, the introvert, and so on. He also describes this complementarity from the point of view of what both he and I consider to be our mission. Both of us are searching for something beyond us which can give a value to what we do.

Our actions have no value in themselves. We both feel this most intensely. But for him there exists something superior, beyond the world we know. He has always believed this. The same is not so for me; he knows I do not believe it. My way to transcend this reality is through action, the yoga of action – *karma yoga*.

I express my doubts as to whether this suffices as an explanation.

Grotowski continues: one has to consider the weight of circumstances in Opole, the external pressures. We knew very well that hidden microphones were recording our conversations. So our language was allusive. We made use of episodes and characters from Gombrowicz's writings when speaking of people and events around us, mixing bits and pieces of essential information with absurd and stupid phrases, with linguistic neologisms and distortions. It was not merely a language in code. There was a sense of deep complicity, of an extreme closeness. We had a common language which isolated us from everybody else and allowed us to understand each other without others understanding us. We could put each other on our guard against certain people who were spies. We could tell each other how to behave, who could be trusted and who not, and pass on bits of information about Tom, Dick and Harry.

The *krasnoludki* spring to mind, the gnomes. That was what Grotowski called the infiltrators, the agents of the secret police and their collaborators, the informers and professional spies. Everywhere there was someone ready to report back to the police. They were omnipresent, in schools, restaurants, factories, in every work place. Also in theatres.

Grotowski smiles. He seems to enjoy re-evoking our past cunning. When people criticised Madame Blavatsky and theosophy, the Mère of Pondichery used to say that God has a use for everything, even stupidity. The novel-like and paradoxical language that we used in Opole became, in the end, much more than a secret code or an expression of complicity. It was a sign of belonging, of a profound adherence.

At this point I note that we still have not found an answer to my friends' question.

Grotowski echoes my words: perhaps there is no answer.

Maybe a part of the answer lies in this conversation, in front of a plate of salad and mozzarella in a bar in Pontedera where office workers and people from the nearby theatre buy their snack lunches. At the next table our Italian friends are eating and joking. Where would we all be on this Monday, May 27, if that young Don Quixote from a theatre in Opole had not breathed a little oxygen into the young Italian from Norway?

Every reconstruction of the past whose memories are not shared by the reader runs the risk of becoming incomprehensible. There are some experiences, rooted as they are in our senses and unique in their irrevocable concreteness of time and space, history, circumstance and anecdote, which only become fully comprehensible through our bodies. When these experiences are narrated ten, twenty, thirty years later to those who have not lived them, the words make sense but it is hard to grasp the implications.

One morning in the winter of 1964, the secretary of the Teatr-Laboratorium 13 Rzędów announced that the *Milicja*, the police, had summoned me. I went there immediately and was shown into a room where two men in civilian clothes, seated behind a desk, asked me politely to sit on the chair placed in front of them.

'*Pan* Barba, do you have many friends in Warsaw?'

The question took me by surprise, and I immediately imagined what they would ask next. My brain began to work frantically: what should I answer, how should I protect the people I knew? I felt an unpleasant sensation in the pit of my stomach and I realised it was fear.

'Yes, I know many people, but I don't see them often now that I am studying here in Opole.'

'Can you tell us who you know?'

I mentioned girls who lived in the student hostel, distant acquaintances, friends who were members of the Communist Party: no one who could come under the slightest suspicion of 'heresy' or who could be jeopardised by friendship with a suspicious foreigner. Why were they interrogating me now when they had never bothered me before? What mistake had I made? What accusations could they make against me? Who were they trying to incriminate through me? I answered slowly in order to gain time. Unprepared, I wracked my brain to remember the 'safest' people.

'And who else do you know?'

Making another effort, I named some actors I had met at the SPATIF Club, my teachers at the theatre school, a few foreigners who had left Poland. There was a long silence. The two men looked at me as though the interrogation was over.

'Do you know A. B.?'

'Oh, yes.'

'Why didn't you mention him?'

'It slipped my mind.'

'Do you know C. D.?'

'Yes, I do.'

'Your memory doesn't seem to be very good. And S. T., G. H., E. E.? Do you remember them?'

I realised that they KNEW everything, every person I had met, what we had talked about.

'*Pan* Barba, we have no intention of creating problems for you or your friends. This is purely a routine check. Do you know P. G.?'

'Yes.'

'When did you last see him?'

I was surprised that I could clearly remember the time and place. I told them.

'He was not with N. P. by any chance?'

At five o'clock in the afternoon when they let me go, I had answered all their questions. For seven hours. On the way back to the Teatr-Laboratorium 13 Rzędów, I went over them all again in my mind. I tried to reassure myself that my answers were harmless. But what is harmless and what can break your back, or that of the person dearest to you, in the kingdom of the gnomes?

In the fifties, as an immigrant in Norway, I often had the same dream. It was night and I was crawling along on the ground with Eigil, my boss in the welder's workshop. We helped each other to slip under the barbed wire without catching it on our prisoners' uniforms. We were escaping from a German concentration camp. Then the dogs began to bark and we were caught in the beam of the searchlights. I awoke and was faced with the question which haunted me at the time: what would I have done in Auschwitz? Would I have collaborated and survived as a kapo? Would I have given up and ended as a 'muslim'? Or would I have joined the resistance?

The interrogation by the *Milicja* in Opole did not have any tragic consequences. It is true that not long afterwards I was refused a visa to return to Poland, but my life and dignity were intact. However, my body remembered the conditions of life for those men and women who defended what was essential. And the essential, at times, was reduced to not collaborating with the gnomes.

Poland taught me that too, and that also belongs to my origins and to the memory which guides Odin Teatret. How can one explain it to those who wander through the fairs of art and theatre, who are struck by amnesia, or who only know the world of the free market with no frontiers? I think of the words of Tadeusz Borowski that Grotowski chose as a motto for *Akropolis*: 'We will leave behind us only scrap iron and the hollow, mocking laughter of generations'.

But what you must do, you must do, and ask no questions.

A Few is the Right Number

We are all children of somebody's work. We may delude ourselves that we have no masters, that no personality has influenced us, proudly affirming that our originality is nourished by the anonymous and democratic teaching in the schools of our industrial civilisation. Or else we can acknowledge in a few people the origin of the path that has led us to ourselves and which others call a 'professional biography'.

Many of my masters never knew me and did not choose me as a disciple. They were already dead when I started out and what they did and wrote was not directed at me. From an objective point of view this can be verified, although it is not true. Their whole life and work was the compilation of an enigmatic message addressed exclusively to me. I spend my life trying to decipher that message which has made its home in my body and my soul, keeping them alive.

All my travels and encounters had been detours on the road leading me to Opole.

Today when I go and visit Grotowski in Pontedera in his simple and colourless room imbued with the smell of old pipe tobacco and whose walls are covered with the books that he has always loved, when I see him sitting in his rocking chair, deep in thought, a line by Góngora springs to mind: 'Who will tell me whether, in God's secret archives, there are the letters of my name?'

We chat like two Gombrowicz characters, or like two old men who already have one foot in another universe. Outside it is dark and time passes with the same speed and the same slow pace as it did when we were in Opole. Just as we did then, we talk of passing events, of the books we have read, of a meeting with a friend. We exchange thoughts, edifying episodes, paradoxes and jokes, silences. The Thousand and One Nights continue. The two Sheherezades remain undaunted while outside the world changes.

Next time I shall tell him the story about the man who crossed a park every day on his way to work and there, in the very centre, was a tall tree with a golden apple hanging from the highest branch. Every day the man laughed at himself, at his senses that were deceiving him, at his desire to climb the tree and pick the fruit that was just a mirage. How the other passers-by would have mocked him ... Each day he crossed the park and the apple still hung there on the topmost branch. Then he read in the newspaper that someone had found a solid gold apple on a tree right in the centre of the town. The journalist did not believe the story until he had held the apple in his hands. The article concluded: some people are truly lucky.

We will have a good laugh, sip a little of the armagnac that I have brought him, and I will feel tenderness and the wish to protect him as if he were an inexperienced adolescent or a very old man made of crystal who at any minute might break into a thousand pieces. We will discover once more the free and easy humour of our hitchhiking days when we were picked up by the secretary of the Communist Party. This too is a bond which unites me to Jurek: the pleasure of the road you follow by escaping from it.

I think back to those thirty months spent in Opole with Grotowski, Flaszen, Gurawski, Krygier, Szajna, Molik, Mirecka, Jahołkowski, Cynkutis, Bielski, Cieślak and Komorowska in that room of eighty square metres that became my homeland. I think of Polish friends, those who were intimate and those who were merely acquaintances, who stood by me with their generosity, their strength of spirit, their irony. I think of the film, *Ashes and Diamonds*, which I went to see by chance, and of the lines by Cyprian Norwid that inspired the title:

> *Like a tarred torch that blazes*
> *you scatter crackling sparks around.*
> *Do you at least know if by burning you will be set free,*
> *or are hastening the downfall of everything that was yours?*
> *Will your only remains be a handful of ashes*
> *swept away by the storm, or will a starry diamond*
> *be found in the midst of the ashes,*
> *promise and pledge of eternal victory?*

A few years are enough for a man to be born, die and be born again. Sometimes a few is the right number.

II

DEAR KIM

26 letters from Jerzy Grotowski to Eugenio Barba

LETTER 1

Handwritten letter, on paper headed 'Teatr-Laboratorium 13 Rzędów', addressed to 'Damfaret 60, Oslo, Norway'.

Opole, 10 July 1963

Dear Kim[1],

Here is your Lama, writing you a letter with trembling hand to bless the Chela[2] on distant roads. May India be benign to you and may that land of secrets choose, among the vagabonds, to reveal them all to you[3].

The Indias of Nagarjuna[4] and the Tantras[5] are in your soul, dear Chela, in your searching soul – this is what the old Lama wanted to tell you while, bewildered, he stands here in the midst of the abundant harvest gathered during his own journey.

[1] Kim, the protagonist of Kipling's novel of the same name, accompanies and protects an elderly Tibetan Lama on the roads of India. But during this pilgrimage in search of the river of salvation, Kim also collects information and carries messages for the British Secret Service. Lama and Kim were two of the many names by which Grotowski and I called each other in our conversations. When he wrote me this letter in 1963, Grotowski was twenty-nine and I was twenty-six.
[2] Chela: disciple in Sanskrit.
[3] I had left for India in July 1963, on a trip that lasted six months.
[4] Nagarjuna, a Buddhist monk and founder of the New School of Wisdom (Madhyamika) whose doctrine revolved around the concept of *Sunyata*, the Void, lived around 150 B.C. *Sunyata* is non-duality, the synthesis of affirmation and negation. This Perfect Wisdom cannot be achieved rationally but only through experience, via a mystic path. Nagarjuna's vision influenced Shankara's Hinduistic Advaita Vedanta and, spreading through China and Japan, gave rise to Ch'an and Zen.
[5] Ritual techniques of Hinduism, involving the transmutation of energy from a biological to a spiritual level. The various currents of Tantrism use the *mantra* - sacred formulas - and the *yantra*, symbolic representations of the divinities and their cosmic forces. Grotowski refers to the particular current of Tantrism defined as being 'of the Left Hand'.

117

And now, dear Chela, why did I not take leave of you when, with your soul shaken by the wind, you left the hermitage[6]? For two reasons. First, because like a good reaper, I had to take care of the harvest, of the hard daily work, before the setting of the sun. Such is the stoicism of the elders, and their way of looking on work. Second, and more important: because there was pain in my heart which could see and understand everything, and knew that you[7] were leaving the old Lama for a long time, perhaps for ever. And the Lama, due to age and demeanour, must not let his pain show. May I be forgiven if I tell you, dear Kim, that you have been as close as a son and a Chela to this old man who says adieu.

Lama

P.S. I enclose a letter which arrived for you from England. I opened it in order to include it in my envelope. Let me know, however, whether you receive this letter; 'à Dieu' and 'adieu'[8].

---

[6] This was the way Grotowski and I referred to his theatre. When I left Poland at the end of June 1963, my scholarship as well my visa had come to an end. However, contrary to my expectations, I was able to return to Opole at the end of December 1963.

[7] As I have already explained, although Grotowski and I had known each other for three years, we used the formal mode of address when speaking to one another. We only began to use the familiar form at the beginning of the eighties. As such forms corresponding to the French *tu* and *vous* do not exist in English, the striking contrast between formality and familiarity in the letters is totally lost. In this letter there is a long passage using the familiar form, followed later by a return to the habitual formal one.

[8] A play on words which also, for the sake of censorship, served to avoid openly mentioning God.

LETTER 2

Handwritten letter on paper headed 'Teatr-Laboratorium 13 Rzędów', addressed to 'Poste Restante, Cheruthuruthy, India'.

Opole, 15 September 1963

My dear Geni[9],

I certainly don't need to tell you what I think of your latest project (another period of work in Poland). You will be welcome in Opole, as in Cracow[10], dearest and long-awaited Chela, whose presence warms the heart of an old man.

But the business of your scholarship may be complicated. I received a letter from your brother (somewhat unclear), in which he writes that a certificate is required from Prof. Kott, but he does not say what type. However, I will go to see Kott in Warsaw, if he has already returned to Poland[11].

In any case, if it should be necessary to take any steps to obtain a new scholarship, it would be better to apply for an unspecified one (that is to study Polish theatre in general, and not to specialise in one particular theatre). Then, once you are here, you could choose whatever you like[12].

I am recapitulating my most recent research: I believe that I could now try – within the bounds of my ignorance, naturally – to initiate you (practically and individually) into the 'psychic exercises', 'anatomy of the subconscious'[13], 'non-private' psychoanalysis, in fact into all the 'Patanjali' of the

---

[9] Diminutive of Eugenio.

[10] Grotowski's mother lived in Cracow.

[11] Jan Kott was the professor on whom I depended for the renewal of my scholarship. At one time, I had proposed writing a thesis on Grotowski's theatre, but Kott had refused saying that the subject was of little interest. Much later, when both Kott and Grotowski were living outside Poland, Kott wrote an article on Akira Kurosawa's film *Ran* in which he described Grotowski as 'the last King Lear in the desert of California' (*Theater Heute*, May 1986).

[12] To display openly my interest in Grotowski and his theatre in my study programme in Poland would have induced the Polish authorities to refuse me a visa.

[13] The term 'subconscious' was by now accepted in socialist Poland and was no longer associated with the idealistic signification that the Soviets attributed to Freud and Jung. The merit belonged to *Euhemer*, a magazine on the history of religions which had also published texts by Freud, Jung, Durkheim and Lévy-Bruhl. Grotowski speaks of theatre as of a kind of yoga which attains a spiritual dimension by physical means – as described by Patanjali – through work on the energy centres of the organism (*chakra*).

theatre[14] (direction, acting, perception[15]) as it has been revealed to me. An uncommon experience which demands a commitment to one's very limits. A true adventure of old Pimko[16]...

Talking of Pimko ... I wrote you two fantastic letters! Typical Pimko to Syfon[17]. I sent the first letter – a sentimental Pimko – to Norway, and the second – a solemn Pimko – to Teheran[18], but they must have crossed you en route, as I gather from your letter from Teheran that you have not read them. You don't know what you have missed!

However I am a solicitous Pimko who worries and hopes that you will not end up in an accident somewhere with that old wreck of a car in which you are rushing towards the Indias, and moreover towards the false Indias if one is to believe that the only true ones are – where? 'Before the eyes of my soul'[19] .

I have written to the Theatre Institute in Budapest asking for news of your book[20] and enclosing many photos (mainly of *Faustus*). So far I have received no reply.

Two articles on *Faustus* have appeared in *Combat* and *The Times*[21]. The one in *The Times* is very interesting. The publishers sent me a copy. It is the source of some satisfaction, although purely abstract. What is happening with your book in France[22]? I have written to the Temkines,

---

[14] Patanjali was the central figure of one of the *darsanas* (points of view) of Hinduism, and the author of *Kriya yoga* and *Kaivalya yoga*, or *hatha yoga*. Grotowski mentions him as though his name was the title of a book on theatre technique to get round the problems of censorship, and he uses quotation marks with all the heretical terminology which might have put the Marxist censors on their guard.

[15] 'Perception' is a way of indicating inner experience.

[16] Pimko was an old, pedantic professor in Witold Gombrowicz's novel *Ferdydurke* and was a nickname for Grotowski, one of the many we gave each other.

[17] Another character from *Ferdydurke*: an eager and disciplined young student. This was one of my nicknames.

[18] The letter sent to Norway is, of course, Letter 1. I never received the one sent to Teheran.

[19] This is the definition by Adam Mickiewicz, the Polish national bard of the nineteenth century, for a mystical experience. It was a quotation that appeared often in conversations between me and Grotowski.

[20] *In Search of Lost Theatre*, which was to be published in 1965 in Hungary and Italy. Cf. pp. 90-91

[21] The article in *Combat*, Paris, was by Olga Obry, and that in *The Times*, London, by Ned Chaillet who participated in the ITI Congress in Warsaw in June '63 and had seen *Doctor Faustus* in Łódź (cf. pp. 70-74).

[22] Raymonde Temkine was trying to interest Maurice Nadeau's *Les Lettres Nouvelles* in *In Search of Lost Theatre* which was originally written in French. This was an important magazine as well as a small but influential publishing house. Nadeau would not be persuaded. However, he published my text on *kathakali* in his magazine (May, June and October 1965).

but the letter was returned to me (they must still be on holiday).

Don't forget, incidentally, that Mrs. Wanda Dynowska (known in India by the name Uma Devi) lives in Adjar, near Madras. She is responsible for the Polish-Indian Library. She is a very nice lady, although a religious type rather like Blavaska[23]. In her time she showed interest in our *Shakuntala*.

And now another address, and a much more important one. The son of the famous Polish director Byrski is studying *classical Indian theatre* in Benares. You can certainly obtain advice and specialist information from him (with which he stuffs fascinating letters to his parents).

His address is:
(Benares)
Varanasi 5
Benares Hindu University
International House
Maria Byrski

Try to get in touch with Swami Shivananda (exercises in concentration, respiratory exercises, etc., according to the *hatha* system).

I have a feeling that your birthday is approaching. May the good Shiva be within you and with you, not only in the feminine form of Shakti, and may he guide you in all haste towards your old grieving guru.

Grotowski

---

[23] Elena Petrovna Blavatsky (1831-1891) was of Russian origin and one of the founders of the Theosophical Society. She practised spiritualism. She had spent long periods in Europe, India and the U.S.A.

LETTER 3

Handwritten letter on paper headed 'Teatr-Laboratorium 13 Rzędów', addressed to 'Poste Restante, Madras, India'.

Opole, 21 September 1963

Did you receive my last three letters, or did your paths cross? Your observations on Kathakali seem to me to be very important (work with the muscles of the body, the face, work on the eyes, massage, respiration)[24].

Our vocal and respiratory exercises are going reasonably well, but it is the plastic ones that are showing the most deficiencies (except for the bodily and facial masks[25]): the teachings of Kathakali could be the solution.

As for the rest, I have put into effect a radical reform of the exercises, and this is based on:
1) the individualisation of the exercises starting out from a defect that cannot be eliminated, from errors that can be eliminated and from the capabilities belonging to a particular person, and this in every domain of the exercises. *Everyone becomes their own instructor.*
2) *the introduction into all the exercises of the imaginative factor* (stimulation of the subconscious). A concrete change in the exercises is already visible.

I believe that this most recent research (self-exploration, psychic anatomy, psycho-analysis of the 'non-private') can, if developed, open up inexhaustible prospects and possibilities.

Even at this stage I feel able to affirm that the 'patanjali of the theatre' (method)[26] along this road is both tangible and verifiable.

Nevertheless I continue to search, although I feel somewhat ignorant about the details and further prospects.

If you do succeed in returning to Poland for a few weeks (as you mentioned in your previous letter), I will try to introduce you to the practical side of all this. It is such a concrete form of knowledge *that it can*

---

[24] Grotowski refers to a letter of mine sent from Cheruthuruthy, in which I told of my impressions of *kathakali* at the Kerala Kalamandalam. These observations became the basis for my article which was later published in France in *Les Lettres Nouvelles* (May/June, July/August/September and October/November 1965), in Italy in *Teatro* (autumn/winter 1967/68, No. 2; and Nos. 1 and 2 of 1969) and in the USA in *TDR - Tulane Drama Review* (No. 36, summer 1967).
[25] The exercises on the facial masks were initiated during rehearsals for *Akropolis*, in 1962, inspired also (as Grotowski told me in 1994 in Holstebro) by Rilke's text on Rodin. Here he describes the erosive action of the wrinkles sculpting the human face. These exercises were eliminated from the training in 1964.
[26] Cf. note 14, Letter 2.

be studied and verified on one's own organism.

I do not know, however, if your project is possible. Your brother wrote that your scholarship requires the intervention of Professor Kott, but as he has not yet returned to Poland there is nothing I can do. If the worst comes to the worst, when you return to Europe I can give you a correspondence course on my particular craft. But I would rather see you in person – does that seem strange to you, coming from Ramakrishna[27]?

You write that you would like to see some concrete results of your work. Well, allow me to tell you: you never see concrete results. Concrete results (particularly in such a fleeting art as theatre) are born and die in the twinkling of an eye, and I believe it is a mistake to tie oneself down to these. Believe me, I have the moral right to speak to you like this. You only really possess *that which you have experienced*, and therefore (in theatre) that which you know and which can be verified in your own organism, your own concrete and daily individuality.

It is here that the kernel of our latest research is to be found: the craft (direction? art of theatre?) constructed and experienced in our own living organism which, with relative certainty, accompanies us.

Therefore, I repeat: if you do not find India in the Indias, it is because India is somewhere else. Where? 'In front of the eyes of our soul'. But nevertheless, I would also like to see these inferior, geographical Indias[28]...

I await your 'opus graphomanicum'[29].

My blessings to Vivekananda.

G.

P.S. Greetings from all.

---

[27] Ramakrishna (cf. pp. 75), the master, and his disciple Vivekananda, writer and extrovert, were amongst the characters which Grotowski and I made use of to speak in a playful manner about our relationship. Grotowski identified himself with Ramakrishna, the revitaliser of a tradition, and I with Vivekananda, the propagator. Grotowski had read Romain Rolland's book on Ramakrishna while following a course in theatre direction in Moscow in '56. Romain Rolland was approved by the Soviet authorities and all his books had been translated into Russian.

[28] Once again it is necessary to remember the conditions in which the citizens of socialist Poland lived and the enormous difficulties in travelling. They could only leave the country on the basis of an invitation from abroad which guaranteed all travel and living expenses. On their return, they had to hand back their passport. During those years in Poland it was not possible to possess any foreign currency.

[29] Grotowski used to tease me calling me a 'graphomaniac' because I wrote articles, essays, even a book about him. Here he refers to my plan to put into writing my observations on *kathakali*.

LETTER 4

Handwritten letter on paper headed 'Teatr-Laboratorium 13 Rzędów', addressed to the home of my mother in Rome, Italy.

Opole, undated, 1963 (probably end of November)

Dear Little Mole[30],

I am sending the letter you requested[31]. It absolutely must be sent together with the letters from the editor and those of a few eminent Italian professors belonging to the same school as Lévi-Strauss (if we really want to achieve some results).

And now about the *opus* [*In Search of Lost Theatre*]. At the end of the description of the exercises there must be a Note to this effect: 'The exercises from one domain should be executed contemporaneously with those from a different domain (for example, the physical and vocal ones together)[32], in order then to develop into an acted sequence on a theme – scene or sketch – making use of the physical, plastic or vocal elements that one wants to exercise on that particular day'.

You won't believe this, but it is true:

1) I am learning horse riding (yesterday I rode alone for eight hours in the mountains).

2) Today I am going on a journey, hitchhiking.

You will see: I shall also become European boxing champion, *panta rei*.

Big Mole

---

[30] In our private language I was Little Mole, young and inexpert, and Grotowski was the shrewd, elderly Big Mole. We thought of ourselves as conspirators intent on digging underground tunnels.

[31] Neither Grotowski nor I remember what the letter was about.

[32] These 'mixed' exercises did not work and were eliminated. In the physical exercises a series of muscles are activated which do not help the emission of the voice.

LETTER 5

Handwritten letter addressed to 'Grand Hotel, Cracow, Poland'.

Opole, undated [probably end of December 1963 or beginning of January 1964]

Dear Sir[33],

How come you rejoice in the sterility of the old guru, and want to invite a string of people to participate in his shame?

Well, a few days ago the guru had an illumination. And *Hamlet* came into being. Perhaps it won't enter into orbit. Perhaps it will be my Waterloo. But before Paraclete[34] I feel no shame.

You can invite whoever you like. *Many* people are better than few. Let me know soon how many places to reserve[35].

The performance is on the 15th at 7p.m. 'And may God protect us and our enemies'.

Grot.

P.S. Please send immediately, *by express mail*, the article by Ludwik [Flaszen] on *Akropolis*.

---

[33] This form of address is less ironical than it may appear: it is, in fact, the normal way to start a letter in Polish when writing to someone with whom you use the formal (3rd person) mode of address.

[34] The Holy Spirit, in the Gospel according to John. Yet another circumlocution for the sake of the censors.

[35] In this way Grotowski makes me understand that I am to invite as many spectators as possible, especially foreign students. *Study on Hamlet* was prohibited after only a few performances. Concerning the desperate situation of the Teatr-Laboratorium at that particular time, see pp. 83-84.

LETTER 6

*Handwritten letter on paper headed 'Teatr-Laboratorium 13 Rzędów',
addressed to 'Damfaret 60, Oslo, Norway'.*

Opole, 12 May 1964

Pan[36] Eugeniusz,

I am writing to you in the Paris-Warsaw train.

Yesterday, from Paris, I sent you a short letter together with the part of
your text on Kathakali theatre that I had not yet returned. Today, on
rereading your two letters I became worried. What do you mean by a 'chill
of the kidneys'? An inflammation of the kidneys perhaps (albuminuria)?
If this is the case, it is the same disease that yours truly suffers from – very
serious if *chronic*, and in any case such as to make your present life-style
impossible. Of all the possible diseases of the kidneys, the 'beautiful
illness' is plain and simply deadly. If it is not possible for you to undertake
the necessary treatment, please return to Poland. I will find a doctor and
financial help. If, on the other hand, you can be treated in Oslo, it would
be better for you to remain there, and try to initiate your work in theatre.
If that is a possibility.

Write to me if I can help you in any way (but I imagine this is highly
improbable). I am working on a theatre project together with J. Poliéri[37]
(with whom, as you can imagine, I have become great friends) who could
procure you a working base in Oslo, but it appears that it will only come
to fruition next year. The intention is for an Institute for Theatre Research
of the type of the ITI.

In the meantime, couldn't you organise something on the lines of the
Actors' Studio? That is, a training centre for unemployed actors, or those
with little work. You would have the advantage of not having to pay
salaries. The actors, on the other hand, would have the possibility of
engagements through performance-demonstrations and studies. And
since the actor's condition is, in the end, a social problem, couldn't you ask
for help from the Norwegian Communist Party or the Actors' Trade

---

[36] Mr. in Polish.

[37] Jacques Poliéri, director and creator of untraditional scenic spaces, who I had met in
1962 and who, the previous year, had published some material on the Teatr-
Laboratorium in an issue of *Aujourd'hui - Art et architecture* devoted to theatre space
(1963, nos. 42-43, pp. 170-171).

Union? It would seem to me that such a project should be more viable than a theatre as such. My stay in France has made me realise how tragic the economic difficulties in the West[38] are for similar enterprises.

My stay in France went very well. Three lectures on the craft in Nancy[39], one in Strasbourg with Gignoux, three in Paris, all by me with demonstrations for local actors[40], in the presence of 'real experts' (experts?) and 'cultural personalities'.

At the Sorbonne, meetings with Caillois, with Lévi-Strauss (who promised to come and visit us), with Goldman and other professors. Pimko in the role of Pimko.

Erik Veaux[41] has promised to send you within a few days the translation of your conversation with me [The Theatre's New Testament].

I am sending you the Bhakti[42], intended of course for people in the profession whom you hold in regard. As for the rest, I will find out what is necessary according to the circumstances. Incidentally, in three weeks' time I shall again be far from Opole and from the kingdom of Alfred Jarry[43]. I have not given the letter to your Anima[44] because I could not find her. In Nancy, Roland is doing the work of two, or even three people, both with regard to the organisation of the Festival and the diffusion of information about our firm.

Puzyna[45] has settled his debt.

---

[38] In the current language of the socialist countries, 'West' meant 'capitalist countries'.
[39] At the Nancy Festival, directed by Jack Lang. Contact had been established by the French graphic artist Roland Grünberg.
[40] The demonstrations were carried out by Rena Mirecka and Ryszard Cieślak who had accompanied Grotowski to France. Hubert Gignoux had participated in the ITI Congress in Warsaw and had seen Doctor Faustus in Łódź.
[41] Erik Veaux, who had visited the Teatr 13 Rzędów in 1963, was Grotowski's French translator. In addition to various plays by Witkacy, he had translated World of Stone by Tadeusz Borowski, a book about Auschwitz which had been one of the sources of Akropolis.
[42] Bhakti, in Sanskrit, means "religious fervour". But neither Grotowski nor I could remember what it referred to in this case.
[43] In other words Poland, the kingdom in which Alfred Jarry's King Ubu takes place (at the beginning of the play is written: 'the action takes place in Poland, that is, nowhere').
[44] Grotoswki's name, according to Jung's terminology, for Judy, the English girl with whom I travelled to India and whom I married in 1965.
[45] Konstanty Puzyna, a highly esteemed critic, editor of the important magazine Dialog, and friend and supporter of Grotowski's theatre. Puzyna succeeded in intervening at a critical moment in the life of the Teatr-Laboratorium, influencing the choice of the members of a Ministry of Culture Commission who had the job of evaluating whether or not the Teatr-Laboratorium should be closed (cf. p. 83). In 1994, Grotowski told me what had been Puzyna's simple tactic on that occasion: he had asked several personalities from theatre circles to criticise Grotowski. In this way they were chosen to be

Still nothing is known about the publication of your book through Madame Saurel[46]. It seemed to have foundered, but apparently my trip to Paris has changed things and it will perhaps be published. Madame Temkine, who will be in Oslo for the PEN Club congress in July, should be able to give you a definite answer.

Nowicki's opinion is correct[47]. So what? Didn't he want to publish your fragment on *Euhemer*?

Of course I will return the letters[48]. At the moment my head is filled more with your problems than the Moi[49]. Right now your problem is *to exist* – at any cost. Make another effort, *within the limits of what is possible* of course, but do it for God's sake. I expect this of you and am full of preoccupations and anxiety.

Pimko.

---

members of the Commission and, after visiting the theatre in Opole, they naturally affirmed that it was an exceptional phenomenon and deserved the maximum support.
[46] Renée Saurel, the theatre critic for *Les Temps Modernes*, tried in vain to get *In Search of Lost Theatre* published in France.
[47] The adjective 'correct' (*słuszne*) used by Grotowski corresponds to today's expression 'politically correct'. Nowicki was editor of *Euhemer*, a Polish magazine on the history of religions. He had promised to print a text of mine on Grotowski, but then got cold feet for reasons of censorship.
[48] Grotowski and I have not been able to establish which are the letters referred to.
[49] In our private language the Moi (a tribe in Cambodia whose custom it is to blind its prisoners, and which captures the protagonists in André Malraux's book *La voie royale*) were the socialist authorities.

LETTER 7

Handwritten letter on paper headed 'Teatr-Laboratorium 13 Rzędów', addressed to 'Damfaret 60, Oslo, Norway'.

Opole, 4 July 1964

Pan Eugeniusz,

I received with some delay the French translation of our conversation on the craft of the actor [*The Theatre's New Testament*] and have only recently been able to correct it.

I am enclosing a copy of my letter to the translator[50], so that you can insert these corrections in the book or in the first issue of your theatre magazine[51]. It is very important to me that all the corrections be made and with great precision, since the correct meaning of the text depends on this. They are absolutely necessary.

Now a few practical questions: I will remain in Opole until 10 July, and then I will be in Cracow. Please, as soon as you receive this letter, send me a telegram to tell me when you will be arriving so that I can make my plans for the holidays accordingly. In short, I await either the telegram or you in person.

Grotowski

---

[50] Erik Veaux. The letter that Grotowski wrote to him consists of two tightly packed pages which begin: 'Dear Mr. Erik, thank you for the letter and the translation. It seems to me to be very good and to have the spirit of Artaud fluttering over it'. There follows a list of corrections, of which I only mention the most significant here: 'p. 6, line 7 from the top: you translate *widowiska buntownicze* by *spectacles revolutionnaires*; it should be rebellious (*rebelianckie*), not revolutionary (*revolucyne*). P. 9, line 3 from the top: it is not necessary to add the word *sémantique*. The actress and the courtesan have nothing in common from the semantic point of view, but only in life and customs. In many places I speak of "excess" , and I mean in a purely literal and brutal sense. You often use the word "peak". *It absolutely must remain as "excess".*'

[51] The book was, of course, *In Search of Lost Theatre*. The magazine was *Teatrets Teori og Teknikk*, which I was trying to publish in Oslo. I succeeded in October 1965 (cf. pp. 90 and 97-102).

LETTER 8

Typewritten letter[52], *on paper headed 'Teatr-Laboratorium 13 Rzędów', addressed to 'Damfaret 60, Oslo, Norway'.*

Opole, 1 September 1964

Pan Eugeniusz,

This is how things stand:

1 - I have written to Christine[53] and am awaiting a reply.

2 - I have not received any letter about the Padua business [the book *In Search of Lost Theatre*]. I will write immediately.

3 - Gurawski is doing his best[54]. He has promised to finish by 1-2 September. If he keeps his promise I will send you everything immediately (they are nearly ready, I will send them tomorrow, 2 September).

4 - I am sending *tomorrow* to Norway the photos of the productions and of the exercises (a series).

5 - I have received the article in French [*The Theatre's New Testament*] and judging by the date, you sent it to me before receiving my telegram. So do you no longer need it?

On 8 September two teachers are arriving from Gignoux's[55] school.

6 - I will send you the Polish magazines as soon as I have collected a few more. I haven't forgotten.

7 - I will fulfil every other desire you may have, my weak character and my laziness permitting. As to the scholarship, all is going well for the moment[56].

---

[52] Grotowski could not himself type so he had his letters typed by a secretary which at times rendered them more formal (see, for example, Letter 11).

[53] Kristin Olsoni, Finnish theatre director and teacher, who had participated in the ITI Congress in Warsaw and had seen *Doctor Faustus* in Łodż. She later became the director of the Vasa theatre in Finland and went to great lengths to get people to send Grotowski letters of invitation. Sometimes the invitations were fictitious and their aim was simply to make the Polish authorities aware that Grotowski was well known abroad and that the closure of his theatre would not go unnoticed.

[54] This probably refers to drawings and sketches of the Teatr-Laboratorium's productions which were intended for *In Search of Lost Theatre* and for the first issue of the magazine *Teatrets Teori og Teknikk*.

[55] Hubert Gignoux, director of the Strasbourg Theatre and theatre school. Cf. note 40, Letter 6.

[56] Although I had not been permitted to return to Poland, my scholarship lasted until October '64 and was sent to me in Opole. Therefore I had asked Grotowski to draw the money and to use it for the foreign students and travellers who came to him.

8 - I can send you a Russian book on Kathakali theatre - drawings of *mudras* and photos of positions of the eyes. There are a few interesting things in the text, for example about the Mandalam school in Cheruthuruthy, Kerala, near Shorapura; on the relationship between the student and his guru (spiritual guide); on the study of Sanskrit and the reading of sacred texts by the student; on the relationship and the interaction of personalities between the actor who dances and the actor who sings; that is all. Is it of any use to you? The book is in Russian, a language that you know well (seeing that you speak all languages fluently).

9 - My tendency towards individuation[57] increases - almost every week it brings me a new illumination on the craft. Strange experiences: I have changed the exercises and, to be frank, I have reviewed the whole method. There is nothing different, nor are there new letters to this alphabet, but I now define as organic that which before (for me) was 'organic', as well as that which I considered to be dependent on the intellect. And everything appears to me under a new light. How can it happen? It seems to me to be such a vast change that I will probably have to *relearn* the entire craft, that is base my studies on this 'organic conscience' of the elements[58]. Provided that the 'Well-beloved'[59] does not abandon his *bhakta*[60] half way through the work. The result would be stagnation.

10 - Rehearsals of *The Constant Prince* in progress. The prospects for our institute are realisable, in so far as any prospects can be realisable.

11 - I have received a letter from Budapest, from Director Hont: in October they are publishing your book for certain. Therefore, if you still have the intention of sending them *The Theatre's New Text*[61] (which I think is essential) this is the last chance. Do you still have a copy in French? Or else you could send it in Italian.

---

[57] A term used by Jung to define mental development.

[58] I believe this fragment can be explained thus: there always exists a particular moment, for a director who is interested in the problems of the training and of the actor's organic presence, in which the criteria that helped to explain and justify appear to withdraw, without disappearing, and leave the way open to reactions to the pre-expressive processes. The director reacts to the impulses of the actor's actions without attempting, at this stage, to define or motivate them.

[59] Christ, according to Juan de la Cruz. Grotowski was rereading it at the time, together with Cieślak, in preparation for *The Constant Prince*.

[60] In Hinduism this refers to whoever follows the *bhakti*, the way of religious fervour.

[61] 'Text' instead of 'Testament' to avoid the religious term, thereby not giving the authorities the excuse of mysticism for closing the theatre, a danger which, during those very months was becoming particularly plausible. When this long interview was inserted in *Towards a Poor Theatre* in '68, Grotowski asked me to write explicitly that the title *The Theatre's New Testament* was mine.

May the hero of Renan, so worthy of being pitied, help you in your thoughts, words and deeds [62].

Grot.

---

[62] In *The Life of Jesus* by Ernest Renan, the protagonist appeared as a nihilist. It was a book to which Grotowski and I often referred.

LETTER 9

*Handwritten letter on paper headed 'Teatr-Laboratorium 13 Rzędów',
addressed to 'Damfaret 60, Oslo, Norway'.*

Opole, 2 September 1964

Pan Eugeniusz,
Here are the photos of the exercises. I am enclosing a letter which has
arrived here addressed to you.

Tomorrow I will send you Gurawski's drawings which are very good.

As you see, the photos are numerous, but unfortunately they do not
include all the exercises as not all of them came out well. On the back I
have written only what might be necessary for *you*. When you know what
the photos are about, I have not written anything.

Grot.

Today I had already sent you another letter.

P.S. Still no letter from Padua[63]. From the day the invitation arrives, at least
three more months are necessary. I'm thinking, at the moment, of trying
Cieślak as actor. Have you written to the *Tulane Drama Review*[64]? I still
have not received a copy.
Greetings

Grot.

---

[63] Marsilio Editori, in Padua, were supposed to publish *In Search of Lost Theatre*. The
agreement was that, instead of paying me royalties, they would invite Grotowski to
Italy with one of his actors to do a series of lectures and demonstrations. Grotowski is
worried because, as I mentioned before, the formalities for obtaining a passport were
long and complicated.
[64] Cf. pp. 63-64 and note 70, Letter 11

LETTER 10

Handwritten letter on paper headed 'Teatr-Laboratorium 13 Rzędów', addressed to 'Damfaret 60, Oslo, Norway'.

Opole, 3 September 1964

Pan Eugeniusz,

I have sent you Gurawski's drawings. There are no good sketches (only free-hand) since Gurawski says that a further elaboration would demand more complicated drawings. I imagine he must be right, seeing that he has done very good work on *Doctor Faustus*, *Hamlet* and *Akropolis*. Gurawski begs you, if possible, to keep the drawings when you have finished with them, for use another time.

Greetings

Grot.

LETTER 11

Typewritten letter on paper headed 'Teatr-Laboratorium 13 Rzędów', addressed to 'Damfaret 60, Oslo, Norway'.

Opole, 20 October 1964

Pan Eugeniusz,

How are things going with you? What is happening with the magazine[65]? Will the first issue appear in English? And when?

And now: is your ensemble of actors complete? What will be your first steps? Do you have a space in which to work? I am not going to ask any questions about your university studies[66] because their continual prolongation and extension is beginning to look like perversion[67].

K.[68] is busying himself seriously with your book. His representative with Marsilio Editori S.p.A (Giulio Felisari) sent a letter to my address and one to that of Cieślak: he writes that the book will appear in January and that he would like to invite us (me and Ryszard) to Italy for that period. I sent him a telegram accepting and proposing - if possible - to alter the date to February.

Right now we are in the middle of reorganising the Theatre. Perhaps we shall be moving to Wrocław[69] from 1 January. I would not like to be away just at the moment when this whole matter is being straightened out.

That is all. Do you have news of Dr. Hont? In his last letter he wrote that the book would be published in October. I am curious to know whether they have been able to make room for *The New Text of the Theatre* (by the way, if the *Tulane Drama Review* wants to publish something more, could you send it to them?).

I have still not received the issue of the *Tulane Drama Review* with my

[65] *Teatrets Teori og Teknikk*, Odin Teatret's magazine.

[66] In autumn '64 I had resumed my studies at Oslo University, where I got my degree in History of Religion in '65.

[67] The secretary misunderstood and typed *perswazje*, persuasion.

[68] Because of his problematic relationship with K. (as can be seen from later letters), Grotowski has asked me not to reveal his name.

[69] The Teatr-Laboratorium was closed by the authorities in Opole because of pressure from the central authorities in Warsaw. The municipal authorities of Wroclaw then managed to improvise the transfer and re-opening of the theatre in their town in order to save it. But at the time of writing Grotowski was not sure of the success of the operation.

excellent *opus*[70], and this annoys me. I cannot show off my qualities as an author and master of style.

A teacher from Strasbourg (Mr. Roos), a specialist in breathing and vocal technique, and a Mrs. Goodwin (English) have been here for almost two weeks. I don't think they left dissatisfied.

Dea[71] is in Warsaw. I have received a letter from her. Kristin [Olsoni] continues to ply us with invitations. She believes in them, but I am sceptical. This however – as you know – does not come from a natural pessimism[72].

I don't understand why you write to me about books they have in French in the Oslo University Library. Couldn't you instead borrow one or two and send them to me (speedy return guaranteed)? In this case I would be interested in works on tantrism and Hatha Yoga from a physiological and psycho-analytical point of view.

But I already know that this isn't possible. You just wanted to arouse envy and irritation in me, just as with the news of your trip to India. The envy and irritation are in fact already present. I shall not fail to take my revenge as soon as I get the opportunity.

As for the title of your book, decide for yourself. In any case, the praise will fall on you and the shame, on the other hand, on me.

With everlasting antipathy

Big Mole

---

[70] This refers, in fact, to my article on *Doctor Faustus*, published by error under the name of Grotowski who was greatly amused by the mistake. *The Tulane Drama Review* was directed by Richard Schechner who, in '64, published an issue devoted to Marlowe.

[71] Dea Trier Mørch was a Danish graphic artist whom I had met at a student festival in Danzig in 1961. She later visited me in Opole and became one of the ambassadors of Grotowski's theatre in Denmark, Poland, the Soviet Union and Yugoslavia, countries she had visited for study purposes. She has become a highly esteemed author in Denmark and has also written a book about Poland.

[72] When we met in Holstebro in October '94 to discuss these letters, Grotowski told me that during those years the Ministry of Culture had prohibited travel by the Teatr-Laboratorium, and this remained in force until '65 when Lucjan Motyka became minister. He had known Grotowski many years before when the latter had organised political protests among students and workers, between '56 and '57. Grotowski, who had met Motyka on a train, told me how he had been invited into his compartment where Motyka had shown him production figures that were declining due to the strikes. 'Is this what you want?', he had asked Grotowski, and added 'and the arrival of Russian tanks?'. Once elected, Motyka cancelled the ban on travel and himself wrote on the Teatr-Laboratorium's file: can travel abroad.

P.S. It would appear that Kristin has unleashed a veritable storm of invitations. They have arrived from:

1) Carl Öhman, Svenska Teatern in Helsinki – Swedish National Theatre in Finland.

2) Annette Brøndsted, Danske Studerendes Fællesråd, Fjolstraede 26, Copenhagen University[73].

3) Knut Wiggen, Rindegatan 27, Stockholm, Sweden (Theatre Association 'Fylkingen', Prästgatan 28, Stockholm).

I don't know how to explain to them that in order to invite me they must patiently and systematically make their applications to our Ministry of Culture, PAGART[74] and the Polish embassy (all three places). The invitations themselves are a good thing, and I use them in whatever way I can, but the rest depends purely on their being systematic and persevering in their efforts. Could you explain to Kristin, when you get the chance, that because of the reorganisation of the theatre (transfer to Wrocław), it is not possible to leave now. It would be all right, for example, in the autumn of '65 if, systematically and without being discouraged, she should propose this far off date and apply already now to the Ministry, PAGART and our embassy.

Grot.

---

[73] Annette Brøndsted, who worked at the federation of Danish students, had published an article of mine in the student magazine in '63. On my request she had sent a letter to the Teatr-Laboratorium on headed paper which could be interpreted as an invitation, although it actually only asked for information with regard to a possible tour by Grotowski in Denmark.

[74] Polska Agencja Artystyczna (Polish Artists' Agency). This was the governmental institution through which all the artistic and economic negotiations to invite a theatre abroad had to pass.

LETTER 12

Typewritten letter on paper headed 'Teatr-Laboratorium 13 Rzędów', addressed to 'Damfaret 60, Oslo, Norway'.

Opole, 29 December 1964

Pan Eugeniusz,

Mr. K. has been to visit us. The book [*In Search of Lost Theatre*] was supposed to appear in February but the publication will be delayed because you have sent neither photos, drawings nor negatives. If you do not hurry up and send everything before mid-January – the nice Mr. K. declares – then the book will be printed without the photos. As far as we are concerned, we sent you the photos as early as September, and I remember you wrote back that you had received them. If it is possible for you, it is important that the actors' names should be mentioned in the book, at least in the captions for the photos. But the list of your faults is not yet finished: you have not even sent him the corrected cover. And now for your punishment: so far your scholarship for September has not arrived, so now it is unlikely that it will ever arrive.

Tone[75] has been here, and she assures me that she has heard in 'very well informed circles' that you enjoy great authority within your ensemble. You are right to revise our exercises. There is no ideal model, as you well know, but everything has to be in a state of continuous change. At the moment we too are going through a phase in the work which is different to that which you observed. Both the way of rehearsing *The Constant Prince* as well as the exercises, are very distant, and also different from what we did before. This does not mean a step back, rather that we are resolving the questions of method at a higher level. In the exercises this involves individualising the training and making the 'task', the actor's line of motivation, emerge. In the psychic technique the process of concretisation has progressed considerably. I believe we are creating a European version of *tantra*[76] or *bhakti*[77] which has its roots in the Mediterranean

---

[75] Tone Bull was a young Norwegian actress who spent several months between the end of '62 and the beginning of '63 at the theatre in Opole. Grotowski had included her in *Doctor Faustus* as the fleeting epiphany of the beautiful Helen of Troy who Faustus conjured up before his guests.

[76] Cf. note 5, Letter 1.

[77] Cf. note 42, Letter 6.

tradition. And I also believe that, at this new level, we will inevitably re-encounter old errors that we thought we had overcome.

If you suddenly made your fortune and became rich, a brief visit here would probably provide you with a few interesting observations.

What is happening with your ensemble? And can your magazine become a reality? If so, when will the first issue appear?

With all respect and with many apologies for being such a bother I have to remind you yet again that so far the *Tulane Drama Review* has not arrived. I have no news from Hungary, nor do I know whether you have sent them *The Theatre's New Text*. Thank you for the Scandinavian magazines. And did you receive the Russian book on Indian theatre and the magazine *Pamiętnik Teatralny* with the articles on us? It is some time since I sent it.

From 2 January our base is Wrocław. The biblical exodus has begun. Let's hope that the promised land appears to us (and to you) at last.

Grot.

P.S. After I had written this I found two issues of the *Tulane Drama Review* and the Hungarian magazines in Opole. I have received the book by Wolff-Windegg – the title is really impressive. I have also received the Anima's[78] latest *opus*.

You write that you have 'heretical' ideas regarding the system of Opole. It is right that you do. What do I expect of you? Not orthodoxy, not innovation. My own present ideas are heretical in respect to the past (those of your time here), and I hope that tomorrow will bring me new 'heretical' ideas. If you repudiate heresy, I shall repudiate you, O Absalom, Absalom.

Gr.

For all correspondence our address in Wrocław is: Teatr-Laboratorium 13 Rzędów, Wrocław 3, Post Box 41.

---

[78] My name for Raymonde Temkine, joking about her relationship with Grotowski, using Jung's terminology.

LETTER 13

Typewritten letter addressed to 'Damfaret 60, Oslo, Norway'.

Wrocław, 6 February 1965

Pan Eugeniusz,

Here I am, in a new incarnation of our destiny: since 1 January we have been working in Wrocław, and from the 9th we will start performing. The rehearsals and exercises proceed more or less at the usual rhythm. For the moment they have placed us in the Town Hall Square (Rynek Ratusz 26). The postal address is: Teatr-Laboratorium 13 Rzędów, Wrocław, Post Box 41.

I have spent the last few weeks thinking back and comparing the past with what needs to be done and built. The transfer of the ashram[79], even without any changes, will in itself produce a different ashram. To continue in the same metaphor: the Opole period is Maharishi in Arunachala's[80] hermitage; Wrocław, on the other hand, will be Aurobindo's ashram in Pondichery[81] (a hermitage-institute that lives amid the din of a big city). But perhaps the comparison with an ashram is no longer possible.

Here we have the official status of institute of theatre research with special emphasis on the actor's creative techniques (and we have also been able to keep the name of the firm). All this partially defines us, even if it is mainly with respect to conventional theatre and its obligations. But how are we to define ourselves to ourselves? And how should the actors see themselves? As artists like any other? As artists different to the others? Scientists? Guinea pigs? Apostles? Or something else altogether? And these are only half of the questions.

---

[79] Sanskrit term meaning a hermitage, an isolated retreat, which Grotowski sometimes used for his theatre.

[80] Ramana Maharishi (who died in 1950, and is not to be confused with the Movement of Transcendental Meditation), an Indian ascetic who retreated to the mountain of Arunachala in southern India and around whom a small community gathered. Grotowski had a photograph of him in his room in Opole. He showed it to me and spoke to me at length of Paul Brunton's book *In Search of the Secret India*, which his mother had given him to read when he was nine. A couple of years ago Grotowski told me that today he still considered Maharishi to be his spiritual master, that he had copies of Brunton's book in English, French, Italian and Polish, and that he made everyone who worked with him read the part about Maharishi.

[81] Auribindo Ghose (1872-1950), the philosopher, who returned to the practices of the Hindu tradition, retreating to Pondichery near Madras.

There is no doubt: transfers of this type always present a tangle of dangers. For example, you can feel, almost palpably, how the work place is no longer that exclusive pole of attraction that it was in the silence of a small town. If we maintain the old working strategy in this new situation, a crisis will inevitably arise and the place of work will become a place of burdensome obligations. The real problem is: how to retain an inner silence there where no external silence exists? How to retain one's concentration in a place which invites dispersion? How to remain explorers, when there is the temptation to set up home? How to conserve the 'madness of the goal' there where everything breathes normality, and where you have to define yourself explicitly on the basis of your status as an actor?

For the time being there are no crises. The ensemble is working normally, maybe even more intensely than usual. But I know that if I don't find the answer to these questions, a crisis could burst, both psychological and involving the development of the method.

As I have already written, the method has entered into a different phase of development which has influenced the choice of exercises and also generated new and often surprising needs: as, for example, the outlining of a certain type of work psychology, or a psychic phenomenology which can be useful for concrete tasks (for technique 2, but not at the initial level[82]). I think I can guess what will be the direction of future research, but only time will tell whether I am right.

Regarding the problems inherent in the transfer of the ensemble and the questions of which I wrote earlier, the practical replies to these appear to me to be relatively clear. But I would greatly value being able to compare them with your present experience. Not only do you know our ensemble very well, but I imagine that in your work in Oslo some of the same questions must have come up, although of course in the context of different conditions. Please, take my request seriously and tell me exactly what, according to you, are the correct answers to these problems. In a way it is a test, and I am really curious to see how much different your answers will be from mine.

I have received a telegram from K. informing me that the book [*In Search of Lost Theatre*] will be published on 25 February, and that everything is ready for the trip for me and an actor for that date. I was very surprised since so far the travel money has not arrived and only after that

---

[82] Grotowski and I made a distinction between two types of technique: technique 1 for the theatre, and technique 2 for inner development (e.g. yoga).

can the passport formalities be initiated – and certainly not immediately. Under these circumstances the date of 25 February is not at all realistic, and I am amazed that K., who knows very well the normal procedure for such operations, is not aware of this. I have replied to him by telegram, but I do not know if it will help. I would be really grateful if you would write to him explaining everything. Is it true that the book will contain additional photos?

I would like to know more about your work programme with the group of actors in Oslo. The daily work interests me too, what the single exercises are like and their rhythm. I am also interested in the psychic problems of your work as director and pedagogue. If you have any photos of the work, I would like to see them. I would like to know what are the prospects of your magazine, and whether you have concrete plans in both domains or whether the general situation does not make them somewhat unrealistic.

I know you will be furious with me and that you will say that you do not have time etc., however this letter-test could also be a help to you, fulfilling a role which is in some way heuristic. Naturally I would prefer it if time and money allowed you to make a short trip here for a couple of days, to our new ashram. If this is not possible, I await a letter, without worrying about how many invectives your mind is provoked into slinging at me.

A friendly handshake,

Grot.

LETTER 14

Typewritten letter addressed to 'Damfaret 60, Oslo, Norway'.

Wrocław, 5 April 1965

Pan Eugeniusz,

Thank you for your letter. The reply to my psychological test (on the conditions of work of an ensemble or Theatre-studio working in a large urban centre) was not included. However, with your reply, you have drawn me a complete picture of your work during this period. It seems to me that what you are doing is right, both as a whole and in the details. If the people collaborating with you prove themselves tenacious, in the beginning your enterprise will without doubt provoke the most clamorous laughter from your opponents. But they will be forced to stop laughing because they will find themselves faced with an irrefutable artistic fact. I believe you grasped the kernel of our research in Opole (and, of course, now in Wrocław): the spirit of change and continuous development, auto-correction and the opposition above all to oneself. In other words, a method which is open, creative, and not fixed like a recipe.

You tell me that heretic ideas pass through your mind on theatre technique as you knew it in Opole. I understand perfectly - it happens to me too. I would be grateful if, when you have a spare moment, you could put down on paper a couple of general points. I am curious to know just how similar and how different, how foreign and how corroborative they are compared to those I myself have brought to the method.

We are already quite well rooted in Wrocław. Many signs seem to me to indicate that the ensemble has adapted to the new work situation in a large town without losing its character of ashram, although initially at the cost of great fatigue and psychological difficulties.

We have fixed the premiere of *The Constant Prince* for 15 April. It is a distinctive production, different from the others. The delay was caused by Cieślak's and my failed Italian trip. And since we are speaking of that trip which is connected to your book, I am enclosing a copy of K.'s letter from which you will understand why the trip did not take place.

Maybe K. has not even sent you copies of your book, motivated by an unconscious feeling of resentment owing to the fact that we did not go. However, if you receive any complimentary copies, please send them to me.

Have you received the issue of *Pamiętnik Teatralny* devoted to us? Do you need any Polish books? I have had a look at the magazines which I could send you, but they are so worn and stained that it doesn't seem appropriate. I would prefer to subscribe to some new magazines for you. Write and tell me which ones.

Let me know when you are to have the premiere of your production, and what your programme will be. I am still hoping, though probably in vain, that you will manage to pay us a visit of a couple of days. A parenthesis: the Temkines arrive on 10 April.

I have looked at your book (thanks to my knowledge of the content I was more or less able to understand the Italian). I believe it has turned out very well and there is the possibility that we can publish it in Poland[83]. On this subject, Puzyna has mentioned a series of books on theatre that he edits, but I would have to add an appendix on the development of the method from 1964 until today. For the moment this is quite impossible as I do not have copies of the book, apart from the one I have received.

As I have already written to you, and as I also said to Toft[84], the money for your scholarship has not arrived. But don't worry: this won't exonerate me from feelings of obligation towards you[85] (assuming, of course, that you care a little about the bond of affection and affinity that unites you to your old Lama, and which comes across with such difficulty in this letter.)

Affectionate greetings,

Grotowski

---

[83] Neither *In Search of Lost Theatre* nor *Towards a Poor Theatre* have until now (1999) been published in Poland.
[84] Per Toft, a student friend of mine from Oslo University. He wanted to become an actor and I advised him to go to Grotowski.
[85] Cf. note 56, Letter 8.

LETTER 15

*Typewritten letter on paper headed 'Teatr-Laboratorium 13 Rzędow',
addressed to 'Damfaret 60, Oslo, Norway'.*

Wrocław, 26 April 1965

Pan Eugeniusz,

I received your letter today. It really made me very happy in many ways. It
is the first, for a long time, which reflects a certain serenity of spirit. Maybe
it is the waiting, and the thought of your imminent change in condition[86]
which puts you in a good mood – although one wonders if it wouldn't be
more appropriate to speak of the good humour of the man on the gallows.
Thank you very much for the invitation to participate directly in the
funeral ceremony[87]. In any case, I beg you to present the Loved One with
the expression of my sentiments and my respect, and the hope of getting
to know her soon in person.

The second piece of good news is your project to come to Poland. If it
really is possible for you, I would suggest the *beginning* of July when we
will be giving performances, so that you can see both the exercises and
The Constant Prince[88]. Up to now two things are evident. First: this marks
the beginning of a new period in the aesthetic of our 'firm'[89]. Second: this
production represents an attempt to do research on the frontier between
tantra and theatre of which I spoke to you some time ago.

This demands an extreme technical precision, particularly with respect
to the actor's spiritual technique; everything is attached to a single thread
and can easily snap. I only hope that this won't happen when you see the
performance. There is the possibility that this kind of work can develop
further. Both from the point of view of the actor's method and that which
could be defined as the spirit of the work, I feel that this is the most
significant artistic experience I have had up to now. And not just artistic.

---

[86] Judy and I had decided to get married.
[87] As can be seen from successive letters, Grotowski came to my wedding in England.
On the same occasion, a lecture was organised for him in London during which he met
Peter Brook for the first time.
[88] The trip did not take place. I saw *The Constant Prince* in February '66 when it was
invited to Oslo by Odin Teatret.
[89] Flaszen and Grotowski spoke of their theatre as a 'firm', making reference to Thomas
Mann, son of a prosperous merchant, who declared that writing was like directing a
firm.

It is always difficult for me to make myself understood by letter, since people communicate much more with each other through personal expression than through words. When I write to people I take it for granted that they will complete the words themselves and associate them with my gestures and intonations. But with the passing of time the memory of the whole context evaporates, giving rise to misunderstandings.

A few days ago I reread your penultimate letter. You say that you gave no sign of life because it seemed to you that the delay in the publication of the book might be attributed to carelessness on your part in the affair of the photos. I am really sorry about that. Whatever might have happened, I never thought that you might neglect the interests of our 'firm' – quite the contrary. At the moment of writing, I thought that you would have read the observation in the light of the joking intention with which it was formulated, as an ironical allusion. The same applies to my last letter in which I wrote of all my adventures concerning the Italian visa (it must have crossed with your letter): all the final part in which I speak of my 'responsibilities towards you', was meant to be the lament of an old abandoned man. You must not take it literally.

Up to now K. has not sent me a copy of your book. I have studied the only copy I have from cover to cover and it seems to me to have turned out very well. I would like it to be published in Poland.

I imagine that you have received the programme for *The Constant Prince*. The resumé of your book inside it deforms and dilutes the true content of the work. But it is the price you have to pay for its instrumental function according to your favourite story: 'A Frenchman is watching you', and also to satisfy the whole ensemble's need for notoriety[90]. On the other hand,

---

[90] At the beginning of the twentieth century, when Poland was split up and part of it annexed to Tsarist Russia, many young Polish artists studied in Moscow or St. Petersburg. A Polish painter tells in his autobiography how, when they had no money, they would go to an expensive restaurant, with one of them dressed as a Frenchman. They sat down, ordered caviar and champagne and, when the time came to pay the bill, they would look around for a rich Russian. Then one of the young Poles would approach him and whisper 'Pay for our supper. A Frenchman is watching you.' This anecdote became a keystone in the 'firm's' strategy. I remember once in Opole there was a communist party meeting with local artists. I went with Grotowski, as though I belonged to his theatre. When the first speeches began criticising his productions, I stood up and, with feigned innocence, told how I had just returned from a journey in Europe and, letting slip the names of the famous people I had met, talked of how impressed they had been by Opole's cultural politics and of how Sartre's magazine was featuring a long essay on Grotowski's activity. Today it is strange to think that small subterfuges such as this were able to ward off the danger of the theatre's closure, at least for a time. But it is undeniable that one of the reasons for the authority's hesitation was the articles published abroad. If they had closed Grotowski's theatre and there had been international reactions, what would the Warsaw authorities have said then?

both the way in which the problems connected to the actor's psychic techniques are recapitulated as well as the corrections inserted in Flaszen's article on the actor's method reflect my present vision of the problem.

As for the reviews in Italy, I can't make head or tail of them. It is possible that there will be a new project for a trip to Padua at the end of May, and if it works out I will let you know how things go. I am not going to repeat in detail all the visa problems which the Italian authorities have put in our way since I have already talked of them in my last letter.

The Temkines stayed here for a week, once again in the final period of rehearsals (as was the case with *Doctor Faustus*), and once again they assumed the roles of father and mother for the ensemble (they made the coffee, prepared the sandwiches, etc. In other words, all-round help was assured).

The book probably won't be printed in Hungary since there is no word from the publisher. There have been no Polish reviews of your book because I am waiting to receive a few copies in order to distribute them. There has only been one article - very positive - in the Wrocław newspaper.

Could you send me a copy of the newspaper with the article about your work? Why do you say that it is the first but also probably the last? I attribute great value to the existence and the professional growth of your ensemble. Especially in relation to the *new possibilities* that you are attempting to investigate.

Here work goes on as usual, and there is no lack of spectators[91]. Your humble servant is working on himself and presents you with his respects.

Grotowski

---

[91] This too was smoke in the eyes of the censors. In actual fact there were few spectators. On this subject, see Zbigniew Osiński's article from 1992 in *Notatnik Teatralny, Raporty Kasowe Teatru Laboratorium 13 Rzędów, Opole 1964*, (Reports on the Box Office of Teatr Laboratorium 13 Rzędów, Opole 1964)

LETTER 16

Typewritten letter on paper headed 'Teatr-Laboratorium 13 Rzędów', addressed to 'Sofiesgate 5, Oslo, Norway'.

Wrocław, 8 June 1965

My dear *Pan* Eugeniusz,

The Norwegian actress, bearer of this letter, came to visit us and would like to get to know you. According to her it is very difficult, so she has asked me to provide her with a special guarantee of safe conduct in the form of a letter, and I am making use of the opportunity to send you a few words through her.

I have received the invitation to England[92], but not the money for the return ticket without which I can't get a passport, and it is already rather late. It is necessary to send the money *immediately* and *by express* if possible.

I would so much like to see you again. But I feel that the price of the ticket could present a serious financial problem for you, and therefore also for your theatre[93]. You must therefore only organise my trip if it does not present a risk. Let me know soon how things stand.

Ryszard [Cieślak] and I have been in Italy. It was a strange trip. I will write soon and describe it to you in more detail. K. behaved towards us like a capitalist shark, to such a point that his stories about money began to irritate even me, and that is no easy matter as you know. Almost nothing had been prepared: the book had neither been publicised nor distributed. I cannot understand why they published it if they did not intend to distribute it[94].

It is possible that K. had not intended to do anything until our arrival. He complained a lot about you and the fact that you had promised to help

---

[92] The invitation to my wedding in 1965.

[93] At that time Odin Teatret was financed by its members: five actors and myself. Every week we each contributed to the rent for the space in which we were preparing our first production, *Ornitofilene*, based on a text by the Norwegian writer Jens Bjørneboe.

[94] To fully understand Grotowski's reaction one has to remember the value that books had in socialist Poland, and the fact that they were distributed - although in insufficient numbers - even to the bookshops in the smallest towns as a prime necessity. In Opole we often queued up early in the morning outside a bookshop because we had heard that one or two copies of the new book by some poet or philosopher would be arriving that day, only to vanish immediately.

him with the distribution and to obtain reviews. Since I did not understand how you could have done this from a distance, I told him so and he became very irritated.

Of course you must keep all this to yourself if you should write to him.

Notwithstanding all this, we held three important lectures in Rome, Padua and Milan and of these the two in Rome and Milan made a great impression. The book was sold simultaneously with the lectures, and with some success. They were, however, the first copies sold (and also the first put on sale). K. insists that his publishing house can only distribute the book after it has been reviewed, but the reviews cannot appear and so on, and so on. I hope that our presence has at least shattered in part this magic circle.

Affectionate greetings,

Grot.

LETTER 17

Typewritten letter addressed to 'Sofiesgate 5, Oslo, Norway'.

Wrocław, 20 June 1965

My dear *Pan* Eugeniusz,

I have received the money for the trip. Let's hope that all goes well and that I can participate in the solemn ceremony of your marriage. A professional deformation tends these days to make me associate every event with a scene from one of our productions. In this case, as you may well imagine, the association is with Jacob's marriage in *Akropolis*[95]. Don't tell your Loved One.

I had only just returned from Italy when a Norwegian actress came to see me. She wanted a letter of presentation for you: it seems that you enjoy the reputation of not wanting, under any circumstances, to speak to so-called actors, and have generally created around you in Oslo an aura of secrecy, even a certain demonism. I gave her a letter, which I imagine she has already brought you, in which I told about our lectures in Italy and the fate of your book. So I won't repeat myself, also because I am counting on our imminent meeting and on resuming those hours and hours of conversations we had in the station in Opole.

I have received the newspaper cuttings. In particular the one on your theatre gave me great pleasure.

What you tell me about the daily training as practised by us and by you seems to me to be correct. For this very reason I would like, next year, to start a Studio for actors, covering the whole educational process almost from the first steps.

We too are now adopting the principle of connecting the exercises by means of a thread of continual improvisation. In this way, I obtain hours of training within which the flow of individual associations changes every day, and from which all the gymnastic-like elements (i.e. those which risk falling into perfectionism through mechanical repetition) are eliminated.

If all goes well I shall be at the Erlangen Festival in July.

---

[95] In *Akropolis*, which takes place in Auschwitz, Jacob, one of the prisoners, 'married' a metal tube, imagining that it was his beloved Rachel.

Fondest greetings,

Grot.

P.S. May I be permitted to remind you of the *jus primae noctis* tradition?

LETTER 18

Typewritten letter addressed to 'Sofiesgate 5, Oslo, Norway'.

Wrocław, 5 September 1965

Dear *Pan* Eugeniusz,

So, how do you feel in your new skin[96]?

I imagine that it will not be easy for you to set things in motion again for the new season, in part because – if I understood correctly – you had to substitute an actress after the premiere[97]. Have you started work again? Are you already rehearsing? Have you reduced the number of actors or did you succeed in finding someone else? And above all: how is Judith settling down in the role of your theatrical Shakti[98]? Greet her warmly on my part.

You know only too well that I combine the characteristics of the misogynist and the misanthrope, yet I have to say that she really made an excellent impression on me – she seems as though she will be a good companion in life. 'May God give you this luck'.

I am curious to know whether you have been in contact with Toft[99], the director of the Swedish theatre school. Can you organise something together?

I gave my lecture in London and I believe the outcome was not bad. Elster presented his film on us[100], and then there was a discussion in which many people participated – critics, theatre people, psychologists, cultural anthropologists, etc.

Your friend from *Encounter* did not show up, despite the invitation.

I made several interesting acquaintances, but the most remarkable is without doubt Peter Brook. We spent several hours together. He seemed to me not only to be an expert in the craft, but also an interesting personality. I presented him with a copy of your book [*In Search of Lost Theatre*], but I spelt his name wrong and only realised this later in Poland.

---

[96] That is, after the wedding.
[97] In June '65, straight after the premiere of *Ornitofilene*, one of the actresses left Odin Teatret to do the entrance exam for the state theatre school to which she was admitted.
[98] *Shakti*, in Hinduism, is the energy of the divinity represented in female form.
[99] In fact this refers to Carl-Erik Proft, director of the theatre institute of Skara, a town in central Sweden. Cf. also Letter 20.
[100] Mike Elster was British and had studied film direction in Łódź, Poland. In 1963 he had completed his final exam with a film on Grotowski's theatre entitled *Letter from Opole*, showing the exercises, scenes from *Doctor Faustus* and from the daily life of the ensemble.

However, the lecture was preceded by episodes which I find it difficult to understand. Either S.[101] is a mythomaniac or else he harbours intentions that are far from serious. He did absolutely everything to prevent the lecture from taking place, lying to left and right and not keeping his promises.

For example: he told me that the lecture could not go ahead without Elster's film, and that the British customs did not want to hand the film over to our embassy. Meanwhile, he told Elster that he had not yet requested the film. When Elster made inquiries it turned out that the film had in fact already been collected and was at the Polish institute. Then S. told me that he had to leave London and would therefore not be able to look after the matter. But certain acquaintances reported that he had not left at all and that, on the contrary, he had invited them to dinner.

Lastly – and perhaps worst of all – he told Peter Brook and also many others, amongst whom Seymour[102] and you, that he had sent me at least two invitations in the name of the 'Royal Shakespeare Company', but that I had not replied. But I had received nothing, and it later turned out that he had not sent me them at all. As an invitation I used Seymour's telegram which he had sent me after hearing from S. that I had not answered.

Altogether a strange situation. If it hadn't been for Elster and Seymour who immediately got down to work, the lecture would never have taken place. As you know, in England these things have to be prepared well in advance whereas, thanks to S.'s mess we had to do everything at the last minute. However, all the big names who had been invited came, thanks mainly to the personal phone calls made by Peter Brook who left Stratford for the occasion. In the end everything went much better than I had foreseen.

We won't be going to Venice. Dorigo, the director of the Festival, had officially invited us and had obtained the agreement and even the support of the Poles. And then, incomprehensibly, from one day to the next, he began to withdraw. First he let us know that he wanted either *Akropolis* or *The Constant Prince*. As soon as we replied that only *The Constant Prince* was available, he began to ask for *Akropolis*. Then when we had at last agreed on *The Constant Prince*, he began to worry the Poles by expressing fears that the anti-religious character of our production might hurt the feelings of the Italians. When this point too had been cleared up he sent

---

[101] Grotowski asked me not to mention the name of this person.
[102] Alan Seymour, the Australian playwright resident in London, had seen *Doctor Faustus* in Łódź and had written a long article entitled *Revelations in Poland* for *Plays and Players* which aroused interest in English-speaking theatre circles.

us a telegram saying that the travel was expensive although we had already established the cost in advance. I am at a loss to understand.

It is a catastrophe that we ever accepted the Italian invitation instead of others. Not only has it revealed itself to be a damp squib, but it has saddened our state of mind for other possible trips. All these discussions about religiosity and anti-religiosity made me think of parochial bigots. In Poland, no self-respecting catholic intellectual would dream of behaving in such a way.

This time I have had to dwell on two sad experiences involving 'friends' in the arts (if you can call them that). It is the first time that something of the kind happens to me, and maybe for this reason the surprise is all the greater.

And what about you, *Pan* Eugeniusz? We met, and we talked for one whole night but still that was not enough. I am sending you a copy of *Odra* with a programme-text of mine which will interest you[103]. Since my return, I have not yet been to Warsaw, but I have not forgotten *Pamiętnik Teatralny*[104].

Affectionate greetings,

Grotowski.

---

[103] The article in question is *Towards a Poor Theatre* which was published for the first time in the September 1965 issue of the Wrocław magazine *Odra*, and was later to be included in the book to which it gave the title.
[104] The Polish theatre magazine for which he wanted to give me a subscription, Cf. Letter 14.

LETTER 19

Typewritten letter on paper headed 'Teatr-Laboratorium 13 Rzędów', addressed to 'Sofiesgate 5, Oslo, Norway'.

Wrocław, 27 September

My dear *Pan* Eugeniusz,

I imagine that you received my last letter in which I gave vent in length to my accumulated anger over your compatriots who took me for a ride. The only thought which comforts me and placates my wrath is that of taking my revenge at the first opportunity (on you, for example). I am anxious to receive news of you. Have you read my text for *Odra* [the article *Towards a Poor Theatre*]? Did it arouse in you the intended repulsion? I have subscribed to *Dialog* and *Pamiętnik Teatralny* in your name. We have seven new foreign students and from one day to the next, just like that, our theatre has become a Tower of Babel. For the moment, we are managing. In a sense, we have in fact opened a Studio on which I place many hopes and am basing projects. We have started collaborating with the Institute of Voice Health in Wrocław. If this collaboration should turn out to be lasting, the results could be most instructive.

What else is new? Work, work, work.

Affectionate greetings and a kiss for Judy.

Grot.

P.S. *[Written by hand]* I have just received your letter of 16 September. Ludwik and I will of course collect material on Polish theatre[105]. Do you already have what has been published by *Pamiętnik Teatralny*? Or alternatively I could send you a lot of issues of *Dialog*. But there is no urgency, is there?

I am enclosing five photos of *The Constant Prince*. If they are published, please be sure to mention the names of the actors – this is important. In three or four weeks' time, after discussing with Ludwik, I will send you a list of possible texts on the history of theatre in Poland.

With reference to your actress[106]: our craft consists largely in the

---

[105] I was preparing an issue of *Teatrets Teori og Teknikk*.
[106] The actress who had left Odin Teatret after the premiere of *Ornitofilene*.

capacity to endure and resist, even in unfavourable situations. You are of the race of strong people and therefore, although I am anxious about what could happen to you, paradoxically I am not worried. It sounds somewhat didactic, but that's how it is. No, I am not worried about my chela. I have faith.

It is true, our conversation in London was rather hurried. What is needed instead is a certain tranquillity, as though one had the whole day at one's disposal even if this is not so. I look forward all the more to our next meeting (is there a station restaurant in Oslo as the ritual demands?). But already during this last one I felt again a so-called 'inner contact' with you.

If they didn't invite you to the reception it means that you evidently don't know how to behave at receptions. Did you spill sauce on somebody's trousers last time? Or maybe you threw macaroni at someone[107]?

Grot.

I have received the Italian magazine. Trezzini[108] spoke with me, but he based his article explicitly on Yoga Sutra[109].

---

[107] I don't remember which reception this refers to. The mention of the macaroni concerns Jerzy Falkowski, our journalist friend, who once threw some in the face of the communist party secretary of Katowice.

[108] Lamberto Trezzini, an Italian theatre scholar, had written a book on Polish theatre.

[109] *Yoga Sutra* is the treatise by Patanjali on Hatha Yoga. It was the name Grotowski gave my book *In Search of Lost Theatre*.

LETTER 20

*Typewritten letter on paper headed 'Teatr-Laboratorium 13 Rzędów',
addressed to 'Sofiesgate 5, Oslo, Norway'.*

Wrocław, 16 November 1965

Dear *Pan* Eugeniusz,

I read with real pleasure the programme that you have published for the
premiere of your production *Ornitofilene*. The only thing which raised
doubts in me was the photos of the facial masks: the actors give the
impression of making a grimace rather than creating a mask, like when
you pull faces. It is a frequent danger in the exercises with facial masks.
Instead, the masks must give the onlooker the impression of being a part
of the person, that the person's face is always like that, or that it is a
customary reaction. Otherwise one has the impression of a deformation,
like in the face-pulling competitions of children's games.

News has already reached me, and of the best, concerning the outcome
of the premiere. It appears that the entire Norwegian press is writing
about your theatre, and that more space was devoted to it than to any
other theatre performance[110]. I am overcome with satisfaction.

Mr. Proft of the Swedish theatre institute in Skara has written to me
about the project to invite your ensemble for the period when I give my
lecture. I have sent him a telegram to say how important I consider such
a project: you can imagine how much I want to see what you have done.
In parenthesis: I have shown the photos from your programme to some of
our actors, with the pedagogical aim of making them feel ashamed; the
fact that you have succeeded in obtaining similar results in such a short
time, with a group of people who were totally untrained, can be a bitter
pill to swallow for our experienced actors.

I imagine you already know about the long review (nine pages) of your
book by Renée Saurel in *Les Temps Modernes*.

Have you received *Dialog* and *Pamiętnik Teatralny*? How is the first
issue of your magazine doing?

I sent you the photos of *The Constant Prince* as soon as I received your

---

[110] It was not true that the Norwegian press took a particular interest in our production;
on the contrary, there were hardly any reviews and it passed almost unnoticed. In fact,
Grotowski, as he explains in Letter 22, had received information about Odin Teatret's
Danish tour of November 1965.

letter in September. Did they arrive in time?

It seems that this summer I shall be directing a medieval French mystery play entitled *Théophile*[111] in Paris at Bourseiller's theatre.

Regarding the issue of the magazine on Polish theatre: I suggest you include two fragments taken from the theoretical texts by Witkacy (*On the Deterioration of the Metaphysical Sense* and *The Theatre of Pure Form*). Do you have them? I also think *The New Liberation* by Witkacy is very good. From Iwo Gall's book I propose taking the *Reflections on the So-called White Wall Theatre* (do you have it?). As for [Leon] Schiller, I think it would be better to use one of the essays from the issue of *Pamiętnik Teatralny* devoted to him which you already have, rather than publishing one of his texts. Among the reflections on space, I think you should print a collection of texts on the research by Syrkus and Pronaszko, as well as on our own research and that of Gurawski. Gurawski could send you sketches and programmes, although it is difficult to get anything at all out of him: he is caring for his wife, educating his son and doesn't have time to do anything. May it be a warning to you.

I think I can persuade Professor Strzelecki to write this article. Puzyna has a lot of material which might be suitable: in the first place his introduction to Witkacy's texts, but that's not all. On the other hand, I think persuading him to write something especially for you is beyond our capabilities (compared to him Ludwik is a productive Titan, quantitatively speaking). But I could go and see Puzyna sometime and choose something for you from his old texts. In the same issue I think there should also be an article on Reduta, but there is no one able to write one. It is extremely difficult to describe Reduta as a model for laboratory theatre, with elements of scenic metaphysics, with the intermingling of obsessions and ingeniousness, with its high standards of professional ethics. Maybe I could incite Ludwik to do it. I don't think that Kott would write you a synthesis of post-war theatre. Maybe Błonski could be persuaded to do so (is there any possibility of paying him?).

A new, much larger edition of Kott's now famous book on Shakespeare has just come out. In spite of appearances, it contains texts which would

---

[111] *Le miracle de Théophile*, by the jester Rutebeuf, is one of the most important texts in French medieval theatre. The project did not materialise. Antoine Bourseiller (born in 1930) is a director and playwright. In 1965, after directing the Studio des Champs Elysées he moved to the Théâtre de Poche-Montparnasse. His choices were characterised by a taste for the rediscovery of neglected texts such as *La mort d'Agrippine* by Cyrano de Bergerac and, among modern writers, Mrożek and Le Roi Jones. From 1966 to 1975 he directed the Centre Dramatique National du Sud-Est in Marseille.

go down very well in this type of magazine. I would also suggest using the article in which Falkiewicz compares Witkacy to Artaud. It is a marvellous piece - a true revelation - published in *Dialog*. If you don't have it we could find it for you.

The general Polish panorama, historical as well as that of recent years, could be covered by Wirth. I could talk to him about it. However, I'm not sure how eager he would be if he doesn't get paid. If the financial question should prove an obstacle, you could use some of the articles from the special issue of *Sipario*[112]. I believe that in the case of a reprint an agreement might be made with the authors to forgo the fee. Don't you think that a passage from Wyspiański's book on Hamlet should also be included?

One thing is certain. If you try to write a little bit about everyone, the result will be a watered down version. I would suggest instead that we concentrate on research and the creative elements in Polish theatre. So: Schiller as the apostle of the autonomous theatre; Witkacy as the Polish Artaud; research into space by Gall, Pronaszko and Syrkus up until our endeavours with Gurawski; Reduta as laboratory theatre, and finally the creators of avant-garde seen from the perspective of methods and tools rather than vague flashes of intuition.

I really ought to feel offended: you haven't replied to my last letter and I have received no account of your present way of working. I am counting on your immediate contrition and a detailed description.

Here the rhythm of work is as usual. We are about to start work on *Samuel Zborowski* (the most intricate of Słowacki's plays)[113].

It is a fact that we have already created the Studio. The exercises are far more varied and intense compared to the period in which you saw them.

Fondest greetings,

Grot.

Kisses to Judy

---

[112] This is a reference to the double issue of *Sipario* on Polish theatre (Nos. 208-209, 1963) which I edited.
[113] As I have already mentioned, work on this text was to take another direction, ending in 1968 with *Apocalypsis cum figuris*, Grotowski's last production.

LETTER 21

Typewritten letter on paper headed 'Teatr-Laboratorium 13 Rzędów',
addressed to 'Sofiesgate 5, Oslo, Norway'.

Wrocław, 18 December 1965

My dear *Pan* Eugeniusz,

I have received your magazine and it seems to be as full of sound judgement as it is striking in appearance. In fact, I am full of admiration. My
only objection is that you sent me too few copies, so that our actors are
angry with me because they didn't get any. I do not know if it is possible
for you, but if it doesn't present a problem could you please send me a few
more copies, even without the 'mother' magazine – just the separate
copies of your magazine[114].

Did you receive my letter with the suggestions for the issue on Poland?
What do you think? In what way can we help you from our end?

We have received an invitation from Barrault to the Théâtre des
Nations Festival for May '66 – I don't know yet what will happen. I don't
know if I will be able to come to an agreement with Bourseiller over the
conditions for my production with his theatre this summer.

We have fixed the dates with Proft for our lecture at the Skara Theatre
School: 16-22 February 1966. He promised us that you will be giving
performances there over the same period, so we will be able to see them.
However, I do not know how things will turn out because so far we have
received neither money nor tickets nor official invitation.

We have begun rehearsals of *Samuel Zborowski* by Słowacki. That is all
the news.

Fondest greetings,

Grot.

P.S. I take the opportunity, at this time of festivity, to express the wish that
life may not treat you and me with such severity as it did the child who
was (probably) born on 24 December.

---

[114] The first five issues of *Teatrets Teori of Teknikk* could either be sold inserted in *Bonytt*,
a Norwegian magazine of design and architecture, or as a separate entity.

LETTER 22

Typewritten letter on paper headed 'Teatr-Laboratorium 13 Rzędów', addressed to 'Sofiesgate 5, Oslo, Norway'.

Wrocław, 14 January 1966

Dear *Pan* Eugeniusz,

Thank you for your letter. Unfortunately I have to distress you by confirming that I was well informed. Except that the gossip that reached me about your success referred to your performances in Denmark[115].

I cannot understand the reason for the problems with *Dialog* and *Pamiętnik Teatralny* since I took out a subscription for you last autumn. Maybe the delay is due to difficulties in sending them to subscribers abroad. I have already been in touch with them. However, I would be grateful if in your next letter you could let me know if they have arrived.

Flaszen has promised to write you an article on theatre architecture and one on Reduta. I think he really will do it, but it will take time. If I manage to force him into it before my departure for Stockholm, I will bring the texts with me. I am happy so far about our meeting at Proft's school. You can imagine how anxious I am to see your performance. I believe that this occasion may give rise to many possibilities for theatre collaboration and should, in any case, be a fruitful encounter.

In all sincerity, yours seems to me to be almost the optimum situation since you have not only an ensemble but also a magazine at your disposal. It is the most effective combination because it allows you to link the creative act with comment, information and theoretical vivacity.

The negative side is, of course, the still unsolved problems with the space and the ensemble. It is difficult for me to evaluate this at a distance, whereas you obviously know all the circumstances. But seen from here, it appears to me that if the provisional nature of the situation is protracted, this could lead to the dissolution of your theatre and that if you don't succeed in finding premises in Oslo, the move to Denmark would be the lesser of two evils. I don't think that it would necessarily mean the

---

[115] Odin Teatret's Danish tour in November 1965 was organised by Christian Ludvigsen who taught at Århus University. The positive reactions from both spectators and critics of which Grotowski speaks in Letter 20 convinced the mayor of Holstebro to invite Odin Teatret to settle in his town. We moved from Oslo at the beginning of June 1966.

uprooting of the ensemble but, on the contrary, could bring about its broadening to include Danish actors, thereby giving it a more generally Scandinavian character.

I don't know if it is possible, but it seems to me, in theory at least, that you could prepare a performance in which the actors speak their own languages. And in the context Norway-Denmark-Sweden the closeness of the languages makes this idea more plausible. On the other hand, you would have to be on your guard against involuntary comic effects.

Whatever happens, if your difficulties in Oslo are not resolved you have no alternative but to transform yourself into Fortinbras and set out to conquer the Danish Crown.

I would like to suggest to you that if, in the future, you should visit Czechoslovakia or anywhere in that area, you pass through Poland and make a stop in Wrocław, even if only for a few hours. You really ought to see our new Ashram. The fact that you are learning Czech confirms me in my conviction that people who know two or three languages become like drug addicts. As you can imagine, I draw my own personal conclusions from this opinion.

I have only received two copies of the first issue of your magazine. One together with the magazine with which your programme was included and the other containing only the texts edited by you.

If possible I would like at least five copies. I have received neither the Dutch magazine with your article, nor *The London Magazine* with mine[116]. I don't even know if the issue has appeared. It was supposed to come out in the autumn. Do you know anything about it?

And now the problem of the photos. I am enclosing 14 photos of *The Constant Prince*. I do not know if they are what you wanted. Concerning the photos of the exercises during the period of the physical actions of the Moscow Art Theatre, it is a complicated business. I don't have any and I have asked friends who are theatre scholars if they could get hold of some for me, but so far I have had no reply. I remember in the fifties the Art Theatre used to publish each year *Ezegodnik Moskovskogo Chudozestvennogo Akademiceskogo Teatra*[117], with many photos of the school's exercises, according to the method of physical actions. It must surely be possible to find the *Ezegodniki* in the largest western libraries.

---

[116] My article - *A Rift Theatre* - was never published. It appears now in *Theatre - Solitude, Craft, Revolt*, to be published by Black Mountain Press, Aberystwyth, in 1999. I do not remember the subject of Grotowski's article.

[117] The Moscow Art Theatre's yearbook in which Stanislavsky's text *An Actor Prepares* was published in 1948.

As for what you write about the training, what most arouses my curiosity are the acrobatics to the rhythm of music or singing. What is the degree of improvisation in these exercises? Do you demand that whoever does the exercise should transform the acrobatics into a 'study'? Is the jazz from a gramophone record or is it an improvisation by one of those present on a musical instrument? And so on. I am curious to see photos of these exercises, if you have any, and if we really do meet in Skara I would very much like to see them in practice.

Thank you for your greetings to my mother. I was with her at home over Christmas and she asked me a lot about you.

Kisses to Judy. I won't send you kisses for fear of making Judy jealous.

Grot.

LETTER 23

Typewritten letter on paper headed 'Instytut Badań Metody Aktorskiej', addressed to 'Suensonsvej 46, Holstebro, Denmark.'

Wrocław, 5 December 1966

My dear *Pan* Eugeniusz,

If you consider me to be a pig, you must have your reasons. However, I have at my disposal certain arguments in my defence. The article which you wrung out of me by force - and which I hope you have received - was written in a period that was particularly crowded with commitments, travel, guests. Consequently I had to write it at night and, since I had to force myself not to be repetitive and to formulate new opinions, it cost me many sleepless nights[118]. If - as might logically be deduced - my life is cut short as a result, you can claim all the merit for yourself.

Unfortunately I did not have Artaud's book in French to hand while I was writing. The Polish translation, although on the whole correct, presents certain ambiguities which I have only been able to clarify during the last few days when I was able to get my hands on a copy in French. I have therefore had to make a few corrections which I include at the end of this letter. Quite apart from this, on re-reading the article, I came to the conclusion that the first sentence should be cut out as it is too emotive in tone compared to the rest of the text. But I will come back to this at the end of the letter.

We have twice tried to photograph rehearsals of the production on which we are at present working; as you know, we are now rehearsing *The Gospels*[119]. The rehearsals are still at a very early stage and in the photographs they appear more like exercises than proper rehearsals - merely bizarre and imprecise exercises as shown in the pictures. In short, we made two attempts, and both times the results were bad. Only today I received another series of photos, and this is the reason for the time gap between my sending the article and this letter. For this reason I decided to

---

[118] This was an article on Artaud entitled *He Wasn't Entirely Himself*, translated first into French by Erik Veaux and published by Renée Saurel in *Les Temps Modernes*, No. 251, April 1967, and then included a few months later in *Towards a Poor Theatre*.
[119] See note 113, Letter 20. The work had started out based on Słowacki's *Samuel Zborowski*, then concentrated on the *Gospels*, and ended up three years later as *Apocalypsis cum figuris*.

send you pictures from the normal exercises which I think are interesting and which have never previously been published. Of course if you decide to publish them, you should mention the names of the actors which I have written on the back of the photos.

We are working very hard and very intensely at the moment. Zbyszek Cynkutis has come back, and Zygmunt Molik returns on 1 January[120]. I shall be in Nancy at the end of February and the beginning of March for a course on the method lasting a few days. I don't yet know what will happen about our participation in your seminar[121] since, from mid-April on, our availability will be limited for several months by tours abroad. I would therefore be grateful if you could let me know immediately the dates for your seminar.

We have many new students of the 'Frenchman is watching you'[122] type. Literally, because four of them are French. We are being swamped by an avalanche of requests from all different countries, so much so that we may be forced to organise some sort of entrance exam.

The issue of your magazine devoted to Witkacy and Artaud seems excellent to me.

[There follows a page of corrections for the article.]

With affectionate greetings,

Grot.

---

[120] Two actors from Grotowski's Opole period who had left the theatre a few years previously.
[121] The seminar lasting two or three weeks that Odin Teatret organised every summer in Holstebro for Scandinavian and foreign actors.
[122] See note 90, Letter 15.

LETTER 24

*Typewritten letter on paper headed 'Instytut Badań Metody Aktorskiej',
addressed to 'Odin Teatret, Holstebro, Denmark'. It is the only letter written in
French.*

Wrocław, 23 April 1967

Dear *Pan* Eugeniusz,

Please thank Agnete from me and Ryszard [Cieślak] for sending the
cheques for the tickets[123].

A few weeks ago I sent you a telegram informing you that I would
arrive in Holstebro directly from Italy around 12 July and could only
stay until 15 August. I hope these dates are all right with you.

I am not sending you a programme for the course. In your presentation you can call it 'Grotowski's method' or else 'individual
technique', whichever you prefer. On the other hand, as we both know,
I am not yet sure what I shall be doing. I will only decide on the details
of the programme at the last minute, relying for the most part on inspiration, or rather on critical reflections on myself concerning what I have
taught up to now.

I hope that you will keep your word and won't overburden me with
work because I am very tired and am not in good physical form. But
what you have proposed seems workable to me.

I am happy to be seeing you again soon. It seems that we have both
had many new experiences of which we can talk for many hours.

We now have ten regular students here, whereas the Polish
ensemble consists of fifteen people. As you see, the happy days of
'chamber' work belong to the past. We are in the final stages of
rehearsals of the *Gospels* and at the same time we are restaging
Akropolis.

Zbyszek [Cynkutis] and Zygmunt [Molik] have come back to us. In
June we shall probably be at the 'Holland Festival', at the beginning of
July in Spoleto, Italy, and in September '67 in Yugoslavia. In June I shall
be in Canada for a lecture. Towards the end of the year I shall be
holding courses both in France and the United States.

---

[123] Agnete Strøm, in charge of administration at Odin Teatret, had sent the travel money
for Grotowski and Cieślak for our summer seminar.

What else can I tell you? I am writing a book. That seems to be all.

I want so much to see you again, and am really happy about our next meeting.

Give Judy a truly affectionate hug from me. For your group, who is so kind, greetings from their 'grandfather'.

My best regards to you, and see you soon.

Grot.

LETTER 25

Handwritten postcard, addressed to 'Odin Teatret, Postbox 118, Holstebro, Denmark'.

Belgrade, 21 September 1967

Pan Eugeniusz,

I returned satisfied from Iran and came immediately to Yugoslavia because the tour had been put forward. Here it turns out that my presence is necessary up until the 25th, which will delay my work on the book [*Towards a Poor Theatre*] since I have left all the material behind in Wrocław. As soon as I get back I will get down to it, but I can't promise any great speed as my state of health is very precarious. I am seriously ill. My difficulties with the food in Denmark, as well as everything else, were symptoms of an old problem. I am now following a draconian diet and consume huge quantities of medicine, but I probably won't be able to avoid hospital and perhaps a serious operation [124]. It really is a joke: we talked together about illnesses in quite another context and suddenly, just like that, we became prophets. I am trying to postpone the hospital, and hoping that things will put themselves right. But it is not easy.

How are Judith and Emanuele [125]?

I embrace you all.

Grotowski.

---

[124] He refers to an operation of the pancreas.
[125] My eldest son.

LETTER 26

Handwritten letter on paper headed 'The Great Eastern Hotel', Calcutta, addressed to 'Odin Teatret, Postbox 118, Holstebro, Denmark'.

Calcutta, 10 August 1969

My dear *Pan* Eugeniusz,

It has been a beautiful trip so far, really extraordinary. Calcutta has just been a base; there is not much to see. But I went to the shrine of Ramakrishna which you told me about. I also met the most important Baul master (yoga through song and dance), who devotes himself to many of the same things as I do - the anatomy of the actor. It is amazing to see how certain aspects of the craft are objective. He told me that since the death of his father who (as is the family tradition) had been his guru, he had not met anyone who was so well acquainted with these things as me. At the beginning we talked with the help of a translator, but very soon that was no longer necessary: gestures were sufficient together with a few words of English (which he hardly knows better than me) and a few of Sanskrit. I have to admit to being proud of his recognition although I tell myself that I am reacting like a child. He was a true juggler of Notre Dame[126]. But at a very high level.

I have been in the Himalayas, near Mount Everest and Annapurna, although of course not as high. I have visited a few holy places, among them the 'Częstochowa' of the Shivaists[127], about ten kilometres from Calcutta, and there I saw the temperature and the authenticity of people's religious reactions, and the fervour of these reactions. Perhaps something of this kind can only be encountered here. I have been to Bubhaneswar and Konorak (to the Black Temple). I came back today and this evening I

---

[126] This was a story that Grotowski and I used as a yardstick to judge people: in medieval times a juggler decides to retreat to a monastery. The other monks know Latin and Greek, they transcribe manuscripts in elegant handwriting and imperviously discuss theological questions. He works as a scullery-boy in the kitchen. At night he gets up and, in the empty church before the statue of the Virgin Mary, he does the only thing at which he excels: he juggles with five balls. One night the prior comes upon him and, scandalised, is about to reprimand him when suddenly the Virgin Mary climbs down from her pedestal and wipes the brow of the juggler with her cloak. *The Juggler of Notre Dame* is an anonymous *fabliau* from the twelfth or thirteenth century and has been retold in modern times by Anatole France.
[127] The cathedral in Częstochowa, Poland, is the home of the Black Madonna, the national religious symbol of the Poles.

leave again for Bodh-Gaya, the place where Buddha meditated under that famous tree and where he became 'Buddha'[128], Benares, Kajuraho, New Delhi and, if I manage it, Kashmir. It has been a wonderful holiday up until now. But I have some regrets because I think I have really exploited you financially too much this time[129]. In addition I am worried about whether you have succeeded in solving all the problems caused by my course in Holstebro (the Danish journalist, Ludvigsen, and your ensemble; as far as the ensemble is concerned, what happened may perhaps have helped to clarify the positions of its members[130]).

So far I have not received the transcriptions from Marianne[131] and today I have to leave the hotel in Calcutta. I am leaving my address in New Delhi and they have promised to forward any letters to me. The last day of my stay in New Delhi will probably be the evening of 16 August or the morning of the 17th. I leave for Poland on the 17th (I have to be in Wrocław on the evening of the 18th).

If the transcription does not reach me in Delhi, it will be returned either to you or to Marianne, according to the address on the back of the envelope. If returned to Marianne, ask her to send it on to you *and then keep it*. The same goes for all letters in my name which arrive at your address. I will collect them at the first opportunity or else I will contact you and tell you where and when to send them[132].

Just a few things about the English and American edition [of *Towards a Poor Theatre*], and any possible future translations (French, German, etc.). I imagine you remember them, but just to be on the safe side I am noting them down:

1) Your edition should always be used as a model[133], emphasising the

---

[128] Literally: 'the enlightened one'.
[129] In socialist Poland Grotowski could not change Polish money into foreign currency in order to travel abroad. For this reason his trip to India depended on economic help.
[130] At that time Grotowski's courses were very hard, both for the participants and the organisers. The episodes to which Grotowski alludes concern a Danish critic who was so scandalised by the 'lager discipline' that he left the course, for which he had paid. And he was not the only one. Then there was Christian Ludvigsen, Odin Teatret's literary advisor, who was not allowed into the working room because he arrived a few seconds late (the doors were locked from the inside). Finally there was the bewilderment of some of my actors before such intransigence and the violent reactions of some of the participants.
[131] Marianne Ahrne, who is Swedish, subsequently became an acclaimed writer and film director. She filmed *Ferai*, Odin Teatret's third production, and made a few documentaries on Grotowski's activity. She had participated in three seminars with Grotowski and was transcribing his final speech of the last working session.
[132] To prevent the letters falling into the hands of the censors.
[133] Odin Teatret's original edition in English published in 1968.

merits of Gurawski and with captions underneath the drawings.

2) At the end of Brook's preface there must be a note saying where it was first published - he wrote and told me that this was important to him.

3) On the jacket flap of your edition, the caption under my photo mentions my 'discoveries in the field of theatre architecture' - this is not fair to Gurawski, as I already reminded you in Aix[134]. Other publishers will certainly write their own information on the jacket, but they can also take this from your edition. Please write that I have requested that the information must be correct. Tell every publisher who has still not printed the book. I am sorry to be a nuisance. Maybe everything is already arranged?

4) It is absolutely necessary that I check the French translation. As things stand, I think it is best that Erik [Veaux] should not be the one to do the translation. What do you think about it?

5) Copies of every edition for the author.

Please could you get me that medicine (sleeping pills) this autumn, when I shall be on tour. I will tell you where to send it. Also the medicine Pancreatinum of which you wrote, but that is less important. *The first, however, is essential*[135].

Pan Eugeniusz, your production [Ferai] is very beautiful and this makes my heart lighter. You are very dear to me.

I believe that my last seminar in Holstebro (the last in every sense) was an important sign. Objectively. It is also a sign for me. Whatever awaits me is not going to be easy, and I pray that I will be up to it.

Tomorrow I complete my thirty-sixth year and enter the thirty-seventh. Youth is past. It hasn't been bad. What is changed in me? I was probably an old man and a child at the same time. But now, as an old man, I say: the world has changed even more. May it be granted to me, when the time comes, to leave it with dignity.

Fondest greetings. My belief in you is profound.

---

[134] During a seminar of mine together with Torgeir Wethal in 1968.

[135] Grotowski had asked me to obtain some poison for him. The political situation in Poland had become particularly oppressive following the Polish participation in the invasion of Czechoslovakia in 1968 and a violent anti-Zionist campaign (in reality, anti-semitic) which had caused the few Jews remaining in Poland after the extermination during the Second World War to flee abroad. Grotowski spoke to me of it as a policy built on 'spit, mud and blood'. He was afraid of being arrested and that imprisonment, and perhaps physical violence, would not allow him to retain his dignity to the end.

Grot.

Kisses to Judith, the children and the ensemble.

P.S. My address in New Delhi (until 16-17 August) is: Janpath Hotel, New Delhi.

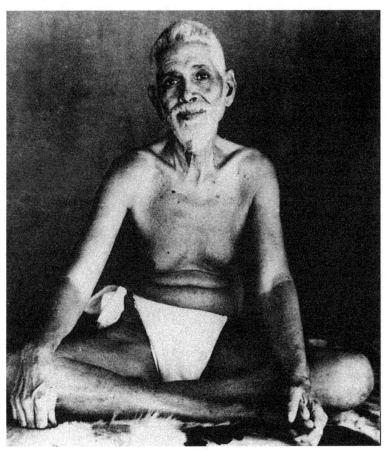

Figure 1 : Ramana Maharishi (?-1950)

Figure 2 : Ramakrishna (1834-1886)

Figure 3 : From the left: Ludwik Flaszen, Jerzy Gurawski and Jerzy Grotowski. This photo was taken by Mike Elster in the spring of 1963 during the shooting of his film List z Opole (Letter from Opole), a documentary on The Theatre Laboratory of the 13 Rows.

Zbigniew Cybulski in the final scene of Ashes and Diamonds *(1958) by Andrzej Wajda*

Adamov, Arthur 101
Advaita Vedanta 48
Ahrne, Marianne 96n, 97n, 170
Aix en Provence: Centre Théâtral 67
Akropolis 30, 34, 35, 36, 37, 39, 40, 41,
  43n, 46, 47, 53n, 56, 57, 59, 60, 61,
  63, 82, 92, 98, 101, 112, 122n, 125,
  127n, 134, 150, 153, 166
Alkazi, Ebrahim 76
Andrzejewski, Jerzy 17, 51
Antoine, André 40
Apocalypsis cum figuris 41, 102, 103,
  159n, 164n
Apotheloz, Antoine 65
Armia Krajowa 83
Armia Ludowa 83n
Arrabal, Fernando 63, 101
Artaud, Antonin 55-6, 66, 73n, 159,
  164, 165
Atatürk (Mustafa Kemal) 48
Aurobindo Ghose 140
Axer, Erwin 17, 18n

Babel, Isaac 79
Bablet, Denis 66
Bacci, Roberto 109
Bachelard, Gaston 50
Barba, Emanuele 168
Barba, Judy 70, 71, 72, 73, 74, 76, 89,
  94, 98, 127n, 145n, 152, 155, 159,
  163, 167, 168, 172
Barba, Vera 48, 64
Barrault, Jean-Louis 73, 92, 160
Beckett, Samuel 40, 85, 101
Bene, Carmelo 64
Benjamin, Walter 11-12
Bentley, Eric 98
Bereza, Henryk 17
Berg, Martin 100, 102
Berger, René 65
Bergerac, Cyrano de 158n
Bergman, Ingmar 94
Berliner Ensemble 94
Białoszewski, Miron 17, 21, 70
Biasini, Emile 70, 71
Bielski, Andrzej 31, 114
Billetdoux, François 66
Biström, Lars 36

Bjørneboe, Jens 67, 89, 148n
Bjørneboe, Tone 89
Blavatsky, Elena Petrovna 110, 121
Blin, Roger 66
Blixen, Karen 52
Błonski, Jan 18n, 19, 158
Bodhidharma 51
Borowski, Tadeusz 17, 37–8, 112,
  127n
Bourseiller, Antoine 66-7, 158, 160
Bozzolato, Giampiero 91
Braque, Georges 44
Brecht, Bertolt 11, 90, 94
Brie, César 106
Brøndsted, Annette 137
Brook, Peter 32n, 60n, 94, 145n, 152,
  153, 171
Broszkiewicz, Jerzy 17, 18n
Brulin, Tone 72, 73
Brunius, Palle 72
Brunton, Paul 54, 140n
Bruun, Guri 89
Bruun, Ole Daniel 88, 89
Brzozowski, Stanisław 92, 94
Buache, Freddy 65
Buddha 170
Bull, Tone 138
Byron, George Gordon 23, 52
Byrski, Irena 52
Byrski, Maria Krzysztof 98, 121
Byrski, Tadeusz 52

Caillois, Roger 50, 65, 127
Cain 52, 82
Camus, Albert 36
Carloni, Carla 13
Centre Dramatique de l'Est
  (Strasbourg Theatre) 72, 130n
Centre Dramatique National
  du Sud-Est 158n
Chaikin, Joseph 95n
Chaillet, Ned 120n
Chairs, The 52
Chekhov, Anton 44
Christiaens, Jan 72, 73
Chuang-tsu 50
Chwat, Jacques 63

Cieślak, Ryszard 15, 26, 31, 32, 43, 44, 57, 60, 65, 82, 91, 92, 94, 95, 96-7, 98, 99, 100, 114, 127, 131n, 133, 135, 143, 148, 166
Circle of Friends of the Teatr 13 Rzędów 55n
Clayton, Barry 22-3
Cocteau, Jean 23, 52
Colombaioni, Alfredo 95
Colombaioni, Carlo 95
Colombaioni, Romano 95
Constant Prince, The 26, 28, 30, 39, 41, 52n, 69, 74, 82, 92, 98, 99, 101, 131, 138, 143, 145, 146, 153, 155, 157-8, 162
Copeau, Jacques 11, 72, 105
Copernicus, Nicholas 21
Copiaus 72
Craig, Edward Gordon 73n, 99, 100
Csató, Edward 18n, 60
Cuba: National Theatre 72, 73
Cybulski, Zbigniew 15, 18, 176
Cynkutis, Zbigniew 27, 30, 31, 57, 59, 77, 92, 114, 165, 166
Czanerle, Maria 18n

Dante Alighieri 43, 44
Darcante, Jean 66, 70, 72
De Gaulle, Charles 47
Dejmek, Kazymierz 17, 18
Delsarte, François 52
Divina Commedia, La 43, 44
Doctor Faustus 28, 30, 34, 39, 43, 44, 47, 57-8, 59, 60, 61, 63, 69, 70, 72-3, 82, 83, 92, 120, 127n, 130n, 134, 136n, 138n, 147, 152, 153n
Dorigo (Venice Festival director) 153-4
Dostoyevsky, Fiodor Mikhailovich 18, 102
Drabik, Wincenty 69
Drawicz, Andrzej 60
Ducret, Eric 65
Dullin, Charles 52
Durkheim, Emile 50, 119n
Dynowska, Wanda 121
Dziady 20-1, 27, 28, 33, 48, 65, 82, 92
Dzerzhinsky, Felix 24

Eichlerówna, Irene 17
Einarsson, Sveinn 72
Eisenstein, Serge Mikhailovich 11, 12, 37, 58, 97
Ekeram, Ulf 95
El Greco (Domenic Theotokópulos) 31
Eliade, Mircea 50, 63
Eliot, T.S. 102
Elster, Mike 60, 152, 153, 175
Erlangen Festival 150
Euripides 39
Excoffier, Jo 65

Fahlström, Öyvind 67
Falkiewicz, Andrzej 159
Falkowski, Jerzy 51, 156n
Falletti, Clelia 13
Felisari, Giulio 135
Ferai 100, 102, 103, 170n, 171
Feuer, Donya 94n
Fiolteatret 85
Flaszen, Ludwik 9, 10, 19, 20, 23, 27, 29-30, 31, 42, 46, 57, 58, 63, 65, 74, 83, 98, 102, 114, 125, 145n, 147, 155, 158, 161, 175
Fo, Dario 95
France, Anatole 169
Franz Joseph I of Habsburg 29
Frederiksen, Lis 66, 70
Freud, Sigmund 119n
Fulchignoni, Enrico 65
Fumaroli, Marc 93-4

Galassi Beria, Benedetta 18
Gall, Iwo 52, 158, 159
Gallowa, Halina 52
Geraci, Stefano 13
Gignoux, Hubert 72, 73, 127, 130
Giljane, Tore 90
GITIS 23, 24
Giuliani, Alfredo 64
Gogol, Nikolai Vasilievich 39
Goldman, Lucien 127
Gombrowicz, Witold 78, 110, 113, 120n
Gomułka, Wladisław 15, 16
Góngora y Argote, Don Luis de 113

Gospels, The 164, 166
Gösta Marcus (pseudonym for Barba) 18n, 64
Gregory, André 26
Gregory, Mercedes 26
Grimnes, Anne Trine 91n
Grotowski, Emilia 47, 54
Grünberg, Roland 18n, 43, 83, 127
Guillaumet, Henri 35
Gurawski, Jerzy 10, 28-9, 30, 60, 62, 63, 66, 114, 130, 133, 134, 158, 159, 171, 175
Gurdjieff, George I. 50

Hainaux, René 72
Halvorsen, Dag 18-20, 21, 23
Hamsun, Knut 48, 86, 89
Hatch, James 62-3
Heraclitus 87
Herbert, Zbigniew 60
Hillman, James 65
Hind, Tage 85n
Hoffman, Theodore 63
Holland Festival 166
Holoubek, Gustaw 17
Hont, Ferenc 90, 131, 135
Hultén, K. G. 67
Husbygrenda 88

Ibn Saud I 48
Ignatius Loyola, St. 58
Instytut Badań Metody Aktorskiej 164, 166
Ionesco, Eugène 40, 52, 85, 101
ITI 66, 69, 70-4, 89, 98, 120n, 126, 127n, 130n
Iwaszkiewicz, Bolesław 84n

Jackowski, Tadeusz 83, 99
Jacob, Max 87
Jacquot, Jean 66
Jahołkowski, Antoni 31, 57, 114
Jarocki, Jerzy 17
Jarry, Alfred 127
Jaruzelski, Wojciech 106
Jasieński, Jerzy 84n
Jensen, Jakob 93
Jones, Judith *see* Barba, Judy

Jones, Le Roi 158n
Juan de la Cruz 131n
Julien, Jean 70-1, 72, 73
Jung, Carl Gustav 50, 119n, 131n

K. 135, 138, 141, 142, 143, 146, 148-9
Kabir 61
Kali 75
Kalidasa 23
Kamińska, Ida 17
Kantor, Tadeusz 17, 40, 43n
Karavan, Dani 12
Kaspariana 83n, 103
kathakali 76, 77, 120n, 122, 123n, 126, 131
Katz, Janka 19, 20, 103
Kijowski, Andrzej 19
Kipling, Rudyard 10, 33, 117n
Kłossowicz, Jan 18n
Klub Literatów 17
Koenig, Jerzy 71
Komorowska, Maja 31, 114
Kordian 26-7, 28, 37, 57, 60, 82, 92
Korzeniewski, Bohdan 16, 17, 26, 69, 72, 73, 83, 83-4n
Kosiński, Jan 17, 18n
Kotliński, Jerzy 71
Kott, Jan 16, 18n, 119n, 123, 158
Krasowski, Jerzy 19
Kristiansen, Knut 89
Krook, Kasja 72
Krygier, Waldemar 30, 114
Krzysztoń, Jerzy 29n
Kudliński, Tadeúsz 18n, 20, 21
Kurosawa, Akira 119n
Kustow, Michael 60n

Laegreid, Erling 89
Lang, Jack 43n, 127n
Lao Tse 35
Laukvik, Else-Marie 91n, 93, 106
Laurencin, Marie 87
Ławski, Eugeniusz 29n
Lec, Stanisław Jerzy 60
Lecoq, Jacques 52n
Lehne, Fridtjov 86-7, 88, 89
Lehne, Sonja 86-7, 89
Lévi-Strauss, Claude 50, 65, 124, 127

Lévy-Bruhl, Lucien 50, 119n
Limanowski, Mieczysław 52
Ling, Dr. 53
Łomnicki, Tadeusz 17
Lopuszańska, Stanisława 29n
Lorca, Federico García 90
Lubowiecka, Ewa 31, 56
Ludvigsen, Christian 85, 100, 102, 161n, 170
Ludvigsen, Silvia 85
Luterkort, Ingrid 72
Lutosławski, Witold 17

Mac Orlan, Pierre 87
Maharishi, Ramana 48, 54, 140, 173
Malraux, André 128n
Mama, La (Ellen Stewart) 94
Manet, Eduardo 72, 73
Mann, Thomas 47, 145n
Marceau, Marcel 52
Marijnen, Frans 98
Marlowe, Christopher 47, 63, 136n
Marotti, Ferruccio 100
Marowitz, Charles 60n, 94
Marpa 50
Martner, Fredrik 94
Marx, Karl 87
Marzban, Adi 76
Masini, Ferruccio 64
Mauss, Marcel 50
May, Karl 47
Mayakovsky, Vladimir 23
Mazur, Krystyna 60
Meyerhold, Vsevolod Emillevich 11, 12, 24, 39, 52, 73n, 90, 97, 100
Mickiewicz, Adam 20, 21, 47-8, 120n
Middelfart, Willi 87, 88, 89
Mikołajska, Halina 17
Milarepa 50
Min Fars Hus 102
Mirecka, Rena 30, 31, 57, 114, 127n
Mnouchkine, Arianne 96
Molik, Zygmunt 21, 30, 31, 42, 57, 77, 92, 114, 165, 166
Mørch, Dea Trier 136
Mørdre, Hans Jakob 74
Moscow Art Theatre 162
Motyka, Lucjan 136n

Mrożek, Sławomir 17, 40, 78, 101, 158n
Murawska, Ludmiła 17
Mystery Bouffe 82

Nadeau, Maurice 66, 120n
Nagarjuna 49, 50, 61, 117n
Nagel Rasmussen, Iben 13, 106
Nancy Festival 43n, 127n
Natanson, Wojciech 18n, 60
National Theatre (Havana) 72, 73
New Testament see Theatre's New Testament
Nijinski, Vaslav 106
Nono, Luigi 64
Norwid, Cyprian 47, 114
Nowicki, Andrzej 128

Obry, Olga 120n
Odin Teatret 9, 26, 43n, 44, 46n, 53, 65n, 67, 82, 83n, 85, 90, 91, 92-3, 94-7, 98, 100, 102, 103, 104, 105, 106, 112, 135n, 145n, 148n, 152n, 155n, 157n, 161n, 165n, 166n, 168, 169, 170n
Öhman, Carl 137
Olsoni, Kristin 72, 83, 130, 136, 137
Opel, Adolf 62, 63
Open Theater 95n
Ornitofilene 43n, 85n, 148n, 152n, 155n, 157
Ørnsbo, Jess 67, 84-5
Orpheus 52
Orstad, Kalle 87
Osiński, Zbigniew 13, 52-3n, 55n, 102, 147n
Ośrodek Badań Twórczości Jerzego Grotowskiego i Poszukiwań Teatralno-Kulturowych (Centre of Studies on Jerzy Grotowski's Work and of Cultural and Theatrical Research) 53n
Osterwa, Juliusz 11, 52, 69
Ouspensky, P.D. 50

PAGART 102, 103, 137
Palach, Jan 102
Patanjali 48-9, 119-20, 156n
Pauwels, Louis 66

Pechowcy (The Unlucky) 29n
Peking Opera 53
Peliński, Romuald 17
Penderecki, Krzysztof 17
Performance Group (Schechner) 64
Perilli, Achille 64, 67
Picasso, Pablo 44
Picon, Gaëtan 66
Piłsudski, Józef 47, 48
Piscator, Erwin 97
Piwnica Pod Baranami 19, 21, 70
Planchon, Roger 39n
Poliéri, Jacques 66, 97, 126
Pomianowki, Jerzy 60
Popkin, Henry 72
Proft, Carl-Erik 152n, 157, 160, 161
Pronaszko, Andrzej 158, 159
Pulszki, Romola 106-7
Puzyna, Konstanty 18n, 19, 84n, 127-8n, 144, 158

Quadri, Franco 18n, 64-5

Radice, Raul 72
Ram Mohum Roy 75
Ramakrishna 33, 48, 75, 87, 123, 169, 174
Ramanuja 48
Rame, Franca 95
Raszewski, Zbigniew 60, 83
Reduta 29n, 52, 158, 159, 161
Reinhardt, Max 40
Renan, Ernest 50, 104, 132
Rétoré, Guy 66
Richards, Thomas 26
Rilke, Rainer Maria 122n
Ripellino, Angelo Maria 64
Rodin, Auguste 122n
Rodio, Jolanda 94, 95n
Rolland, Romain 75, 123n
Rotbaum, Jakub 19, 21
Rousseau, Henri (known as le Douanier) 87
Roux, Jean Louis 72
Royal Shakespeare Company 60n, 94, 153
Royal Theatre (Copenhagen) 93
Różewicz, Tadeusz 17, 18n, 40

Ruffini, Franco 13
Rumi, Jalal ad-Din 107
Rusinek, Kazimierz 83n
Rutebeuf 158n

S. 153
Saint-Denis, Michel 72, 73
Saint-Denis, Suria 72
Saint-Exupéry, Antoine de 35
Salgari, Emilio 48
Salmon, André 44, 87
Salvagni, Adriana 70
Samuel Zborowski 102, 159, 160, 164n
Sandauer, Artur 17
Sannum, Tor 91n
Sariputra 49
Sartre, Jean-Paul 15, 62, 63, 146n
Sarvig, Ole 85n, 93
Saurel, Renée 62, 63, 94, 128, 157, 164n
Savarese, Nicola 13
Schall, Barbara 94
Schall, Ekkehard 94
Schechner, Richard 63-4, 136n
Schiller, Leon 158, 159
Schino, Mirella 13
Scierski, Stanisław 31
Seeberg, Peter 85n
Seweryn, Andrzej 32n
Seymour, Alan 72, 153
Shakespeare, William 77, 78, 158
Shakti 121, 152
Shakuntala 31, 55n, 57, 82, 121
Shams 107
Shankara 48, 117n
Shivananda, Swami 121
Sieffert, René 66
Silesius, Angelus 50
Skeel, Rina 13
Skuszanka, Krystyna 17, 18n, 19, 40
Słowacki, Juliusz 26, 47, 102, 159, 160, 164n
Sophocles 15, 16, 39
SOSTUD 88
SPATIF Club 17, 22, 111
Stanislavsky, Konstantin Sergeievich 11, 12, 23, 38, 40, 45, 52, 55, 58, 90, 100, 105, 162n

Starowieyska, Eva 17
Stein, Gertrude 87
Stewart, Ellen (La Mama) 94
Stopka, Andrzej 17
Strasbourg Theatre (Centre
Dramatique de l'Est) 72, 130n
Strøm, Agnete 94, 166
Strzelecki, Zenobiusz 17, 18n, 60, 158
Studio des Champs-Elysées 66, 158n
Studium o Hamlecie 77-82, 83, 92,
125, 134
Sulerzhitski, Leopold 11, 12
Svenska Teatern (Swedish National
Theatre) 137
Świderski, Jan 17
Swinarski, Artur Maria 17, 62
Swinarski, Konrad 17, 40
Syrkus, Szymon 158, 159
Szajna, Jósef 17, 18n, 19, 30, 34, 40,
43n, 114
Szejnert, Małgorzata 83n
Szymanowski, Karol 17

Tagore, Rabindranath 75
Tagore family 75
Tairov, Aleksandr Yakovleivich 24
Tarn, Adam 18n
Taviani, Ferdinando 13
Taviani, Paolo 13
Teatr Co To 18
Teatr Poezji 52
Teatr Polski 19, 21
Teatr Słowacki 19, 29
Teatr Stary 19
Teatr 13 Rzędów 10, 19, 20, 23, 26,
27, 29, 30, 31-2, 33, 36, 42, 43, 45, 52,
53n, 54, 60, 61, 64n, 65n, 67-8, 127n
see also Teatr-Laboratorium
Teatr 38 19
Teatr Ziemi Opolskiej 29n, 43n
Teatr Żydowski (Jewish Theatre) 17
Teatr-Laboratorium 13 Rzędów 9, 32,
36, 41, 43n, 45-6, 53n, 58, 60, 63, 66,
69, 70, 73, 74, 77, 81, 82, 83, 84n, 91-
2, 94, 108, 117, 119, 122, 124, 125n,
126, 127n, 129, 130, 133, 134, 135,
136n, 137n, 138, 139, 140, 145, 147n,
148, 155, 157, 160, 161

Temkine, Raymonde 36-7, 39n, 55,
65, 66, 73, 83, 100, 120-1, 128, 139,
144, 147
Temkine, Valentin 36, 65, 73, 120-1,
144, 147
Tenschert, Joachim 94
Théâtre de l'Est (Paris) 66
Théâtre de Poche-Montparnasse 158n
Théâtre des Nations (festival) 70, 73,
92, 160
Theatre's New Testament, The 47, 127,
129, 130, 131, 139
Tierney, Mary 63
Timoszewicz, Jerzy 83n
Tinti, Roberto 13
Toeplitz, Krzysztof Teodor 17
Toft, Per 144
Tomaszewski, Henryk 18n, 39, 52n,
92
Trezzini, Lamberto 64, 156
Trilling, Ossia 72

Uma Devi 121
Uncle Vania 29
Utrillo, Maurice 87

Vachtangov, Evgeny Bogrationovich
11, 12, 23, 52
Valadon, Suzanne 87
Varley, Julia 13
Vasa Theatre 130n
Veaux, Erik 17, 61, 65, 93, 127, 129n,
164n, 171
Vega Carpio, Felix Lope de 38
Veinstein, André 66
Venice Festival 100, 153
Vivekananda 33, 123
Volli, Ugo 13

Wagner, Richard 38
Wajda, Andrzej 15, 83n, 89, 176
Weideli, Walter 65
Weigel, Helene 94
Weil, Simone 102
Weiss, Peter 101
Wekwerth, Manfred 94
Westin, Martha 96

Wethal, Torgeir 13, 60, 91n, 96, 171n
Wielka Reforma 40, 54
Wiggen, Knut 137
Winnje, Eigil 86, 112
Wirth, Andrzej 18n, 159
Witkacy (Stanislaw Ignacy
Witkiewicz) 17, 18n, 43n, 52, 84,
127n, 158, 159, 165
Wolff-Windegg, Philip 65, 139
Wolford, Lisa 64n
Woszczerowicz, Jacek 17
Woźniak, Leszek 21
Wróblewski, Andrzej 18n
Wysiński, Andrzej 83n
Wyspiański, Stanisław 47, 77, 78, 159

Youth Festival (Helsinki) 36

Zachwatowicz, Krystyna 17, 18n
Zamkow-Słomczynska, Lidia 18n
Zavadsky, Yuri Aleksandrovich 23-5
Zeami, Motokiyo 97
Ziemska, Teresa 70, 71
Zmysłowski, Jacek 26

EUROPEAN CONTEMPORARY CLASSICS/
THEATRE is a major series of ground-
breaking, authoritative works by scholars
and practitioners from throughout Europe. It
makes available, in English, new thinking on
the practice of theatre, its processes and
contexts. It aims to document innovative
methods, theories and approaches to
making and understanding theatre.

Other books already in the process of translation and production include:

Eugenio Barba
Theatre - Solitude, Craft, Revolt

Ingemar Lindh
Stepping Stones

Krysztof Plesniarowicz
*The Dead Memory Machine: Tadeusz
Kantor's Theatre of Death*

Franco Ruffini
Theatre and Boxing

Nicola Savarese
*Theatre and Performance Between East and
West*

 Black Mountain Press is a division of the
Centre for Performance Research Ltd.

 *An Independent Theatre Organisation
Located in Wales
Working Internationally*

The Centre for Performance Research
produces innovative performance work,
promotes tours, collaborates and exchanges
with theatre companies of international
significance, arranges conferences, stages
workshops, masterclasses and lecture
demonstrations, publishes and distributes
theatre books, mounts exhibitions and runs
a multicultural resource centre for the
performing arts.

Artistic Director: Richard Gough
Producer: Judie Christie
Publications Assistant: Rachel Rogers

CENTRE FOR PERFORMANCE RESEARCH
8 SCIENCE PARK, ABERYSTWYTH
SY23 3AH, WALES, UK
TEL: +44 (0) 1970 622 133
Fax: +44 (0) 1970 622 132
email: cprwww@aber.ac.uk
http://www.aber.ac.uk/-cprwww

*

LAND OF ASHES AND DIAMONDS

Land of Ashes and Diamonds publishes for the first time a series of letters from Jerzy Grotowski to Eugenio Barba, written during the early 'Theatre of Productions' phase of Grotowski's work in the 1960's. The letters are contextualised in an extended autobiographical essay by Barba, which chronicles his early contact, and lifelong friendship, with Grotowski and his close collaborators, and charts their deep significance to his own life and work. Detailing the precise, concrete, sustained, and measured work upon which the theatre practice of Grotowski's Laboratorium was founded, *Land of Ashes and Diamonds* offers new insights into the work of two great masters of twentieth century theatre.

*

EUGENIO BARBA

Eugenio Barba was born in southern Italy in 1936 and emigrated to Norway in 1954. From 1961-64 he studied theatre in Poland, spending three years with Jerzy Grotowski and writing the first book about him. In 1963, after a journey to India, he published an essay on *kathakali*, a theatre form which was not, at the time, extensively known in the West. He founded Odin Teatret in Oslo in 1964 and moved with it to Denmark in 1966, directing more than twenty performances to date which have toured regularly in Europe, North America and Latin America. In 1979 he founded ISTA, the International School of Theatre Anthropology, and has been awarded honorary doctorates from the Universities of: Århus, Denmark; Ayacucho, Peru; Bologna, Italy.

Of the books he has published, the following have been translated into English: *Beyond the Floating Islands* (PAJ Publications 1986), *The Paper Canoe* (Routledge 1995) and, in collaboration with Nicola Savarese, *A Dictionary of Theatre Anthropology: The Secret Art of the Performer* (CPR/ Routledge 1991).